C000004852

Gift to

_____

From

_____

Message

_____

_____

_____

Joy in the Morning

JOY IN THE MORNING by Selwyn Hughes

© 1998:   Christian Art
            P O Box 1599
            Vereeniging
            1930
            South Africa

Copyright © 1994, 1995, 1996, 1997 by Selwyn Hughes.
A compilation of excerpts from the original devotional booklets published under the title *Every Day with Jesus* by Selwyn Hughes.

Design by: Christian Art

ISBN 1-85345-129-0

Printed in Hong Kong.

JANUARY

The primary focus

In the beginning God ...
Genesis 1:1

*W*e begin a new year by focusing on what without doubt is the most noble and loftiest of themes – the nature and character of God. I have noticed that Christians, generally speaking, seem to be preoccupied with knowing more about themselves rather than knowing more about God. I believe that the Bible opens with the thunderous acclaim: "In the beginning God ... " I tell you with all the conviction of which I am capable – if God is not our primary focus, then everything else will soon get out of focus.

For reading & meditation – Genesis 1:1-12

A lost art

Who has known the mind of the Lord?
Or who has been his counsellor?
Romans 11:34

A subject which is of great interest to many to-day is anthropology – the study of man. Although this subject is of great importance, for a Christian there is something far more important – the study of God. It was the great preacher C.H. Spurgeon who said: "The highest science, the loftiest speculation, the mightiest philosophy that can ever engage the attention of a child of God, is the name, the nature, the person, the work, the doings, and the existence of the great God whom he calls his Father."

For reading & meditation – Romans 11:25-36

J A N U A R Y   2

Quiet contemplation

For you make me glad by your deeds, O Lord ...
Psalm 92:4

"*T*he soul," says one theologian, "is at home only when it is in God." He meant, of course, that as the soul was made for God it can only function effectively when indwelt by God. Contemplation of God is like breath to the soul; it inflates it and causes it to be fully actualized. "My body and my whole physiology functions better when God is in it," said a doctor to me some years ago. I replied: "And so it is also with the soul, dear Doctor, so it is also with the soul."

For reading & meditation – Psalm 92:1-15

"Eccentric" Christians

He sits enthroned above the circle of the earth,
and its people are like grasshoppers.
Isaiah 40:22

*T*he man-centred focus that is creeping into today's Church must be resisted at all costs. I am not suggesting that we should close our eyes to the fact that men and women need help on such matters as disciplining children, marital problems, establishing proper priorities, etc. These issues should be addressed also, but we must be careful that "market forces" do not mould our theology. People may *want* to know about these issues, but what they *need*, primarily, is to know God.

For reading & meditation – Isaiah 40:21-31

J A N U A R Y   4

Stirred – but not shaken

Because he is at my right hand, I shall not be shaken.
Psalm 16:8

*A*sk yourself this question now: Do I allow myself to be more overwhelmed by the wrong people have done to me than the wrong I might have done (and may still be doing) to God by my unwillingness to trust him? Putting the glory of God before our well-being does not go down well with some modern-day Christians brought up in the "Me" generation. It means that we have to break away from the idea that life revolves around our desires, our ambitions, our self-image, our personal comfort, our hurts and problems, but instead around the glory and the will of God.

For reading & meditation – Psalm 16:1-11

JANUARY 5

God marginalised

*... but let him who boasts boast about this:
that he understands and knows me ...*
Jeremiah 9:24

*T*he reason for the spiritual dullness in so many lives is that we have lost our sense of priority. *The world is too much with us!* Therein lies our problem. Other things, other issues, other problems, other priorities have been allowed to press in upon us, and the consequence of all this is that God has become marginalised. Through the prophet Jeremiah God speaks to us and shows us that his greatest desire is that we should come to know him. When we lose God we lose touch with reality, for reality, as one great Christian put it, is Jesus' other Name.

For reading & meditation – Jeremiah 9:17-24

JANUARY 6

"God Himself"

Your love is like the morning mist,
like the early dew that disappears.
Hosea 6:4

A danger that we must acquaint ourselves with as we discuss the need to contemplate God more deeply is that of becoming more interested in godliness than in God himself. Theologian Jim Packer puts the point effectively when he says that "moving in evangelical circles as I do I am often troubled by what I find. While my fellow believers are constantly seeking to advance in godliness, they show little direct interest in God himself. When they study Scripture, only the principles of personal godliness get their attention; their heavenly Father does not."

For reading & meditation – Hosea 6:1-11

JANUARY 7

Seeing the invisible

... he persevered because he saw him who is invisible.
Hebrews 11:27

*W*e all find it easier to *do* than to *be*; we prefer a plan to follow rather than a Person to trust. What our carnal nature hates to be faced with is the challenge of throwing ourselves in utter dependency on a God who is invisible and intangible. Yet this is what a relationship with God entails. It is possible to see the invisible, but it is possible only to the eye of faith.

For reading & meditation – Hebrews 11:17-28

JANUARY 8

Balanced Christianity

> *After beginning with the Spirit, are you now
> trying to attain your goal by human effort?*
> Galatians 3:3

The difficulty with faith and works is this: we come into the Christian life by depending on the innocent sufferings of our Lord Jesus Christ as sufficient ground for our acceptance with God, and then when we learn the principles of Christian living we turn from dependency on Christ to dependency on them. This was the great problem in the Galatian church and it is still a problem here in the Church of the twentieth century. Bringing forth the fruit of repentance by good works is terribly important but we are not to depend on works for our salvation.

For reading & meditation – Galatians 3:1-25

JANUARY 9

Meeting the Person

*I want to know Christ and the
power of his resurrection ...*
Philippians 3:10

*W*e must seek to enlarge our acquaintance not simply with the characteristics of his nature, but with the living God whose characteristics they are. I have often seen students of Scripture fall into the trap of contemplating the principles which God has built into the universe more than God himself. They underline them in their Bible, mark alongside them other Scriptural references, and think that by doing this they are growing spiritually. The problem is that only the principles of daily personal godliness capture their interest; their heavenly Father does not.

For reading & meditation – Philippians 3:1-14

J A N U A R Y   10

God's self-revelation

But those who trust in idols ...
will be turned back in utter shame.
Isaiah 42:17

*T*he Bible (I believe) has been supernaturally protected from the effects and influences of sin, and in its pages we have a clear revelation of who God is and what he is like. This is why all human ideas about God, his will and his work, both traditional and contemporary, must be ruthlessly brought in line with what Scripture says. I can look into my own heart to see what I am like but I have to look into the Bible to see what God is like.

For reading & meditation – Isaiah 42:10-17

The great Creator

... he who created the heavens and stretched them out, who spread out the earth ...
Isaiah 42:5

*T*oday we ask ourselves: What is the first thing we learn about God as we open up the Scriptures? And the first thing we see him do is to act creatively. As God has a will to do good, so he has the necessary power to execute that will. Who can look upward to the midnight sky, behold its wonders and not exclaim: "Of what were these mighty orbs formed?" A great and powerful God brought them into being simply by saying: "Let them be." This kind of God can have my heart anytime.

For reading & meditation – Isaiah 42:1-9

JANUARY 12

A Big Being

By the word of the Lord were the heavens made,
their starry host by the breath of his mouth.
Psalm 33:6

*W*hat many scientists are not prepared to admit is that the ultimate energy behind the universe is not a Big Bang, but a Big Being – an intelligent Being of indescribable majesty and power who is able to do whatever he chooses. And because what he chooses is always good, he can be trusted to have the best interests of his creation at heart. I find that contemplating this awesome, mighty, all-powerful God, my soul instinctively cries: "How great thou art." I hope yours does too!

For reading & meditation – Psalm 33:1-22

JANUARY 13

Sustained and secure

*These all look to you to give them
their food at the proper time.*
Psalm 104:27

*B*oth man and beast would perish if there were no
food, and there would be no food if the earth were
not refreshed with fruitful showers. As one preacher
put it: "We came from God's hand and we remain
in his hand." Everywhere in the Scriptures God is
presented not only as the Creator of the world but
as its Sustainer and Preserver also. If God were to
die the universe would fall to pieces. But don't
worry – God cannot die. The universe is quite
secure.

For reading & meditation – Psalm 104:1-35

The God who speaks

As the heavens are higher than the earth,
so are my ways higher than your ways
and my thoughts than your thoughts.
Isaiah 55:9

*T*he next thing we observe about God is that he is personal. But what does it mean to be a person? To be a person we have to be able to think, to reason, to feel, to judge, to choose and to communicate in words that constitute a language. There is more to God than mere power; the Almighty is a Person. This means, among other things, that the Almighty cannot be studied from a "safe" distance. Because he is a Person he is someone who wants and waits to be "known".

For reading & meditation – Isaiah 55:1-13

JANUARY 15

Plenty of time for you

*How precious to me are your thoughts,
O God! How vast is the sum of them!*
Psalm 139:17

*W*hile it is said that the majority of human beings believe in some kind of God, many view him
as being so great and infinite that he cannot possibly take a personal interest in such small and
insignificant creatures as ourselves. Dr Henry
Norris Russell, one of the great astronomers of
this century and a Christian, once gave a talk on
the vastness of the universe. Afterwards someone
asked him this question: "How is it possible for
such a great and infinite God to have time for me?"
This was his reply: "An infinite God can dispatch
the affairs of this universe in the twinkling of an
eye, thus giving him plenty of time for you."

For reading & meditation – Psalm 139:1-24

JANUARY   16

God is Three

*I urge you ... by our Lord Jesus Christ and by the
love of the Spirit ... by praying to God ...*
Romans 15:30

"*G*od is One, yet God is Three. How can such
a strange thing be?" These are the lines of a ditty
that supposedly was sung by troops on the march
in World War I. Basically the doctrine of the
Trinity is this: God is One but with three distinct
centres of consciousness. What we must see, is
that no words can fully explain the truth of the
Trinity. We use the term "Trinity" expecting not
so much that in that one word the truth may be
spoken, but that it may not be left unspoken.

For reading & meditation – Romans 15:23-30

Logically necessary

Give thanks to the God of gods.
His love endures for ever.
Psalm 136:2

*I*t must be noted though that it is not only in isolated texts that one encounters the doctrine of the Trinity. Love, to be love, must have an object. Self-love is love's opposite. Since God is *eternal* love, he must have had objects of eternal affection. The objects of his affection were the Son and the Spirit. The doctrine of the Trinity, therefore, is not only theologically but logically necessary to an understanding of the nature of the Deity.

For reading & meditation – Psalm 136:1-26

JANUARY 18

The great triune God

Thomas said to him, "My Lord and my God!"
John 20:28

*T*he best argument I am aware of for the Trinity is this. God, we know, is one God. But there stepped into the world one day someone who claimed also to be God. He came from Nazareth and his name was Jesus. He forgave sins, claimed to have existence before Abraham, and accepted worship as his right. After Jesus was resurrected and returned to heaven he sent back the Holy Spirit – the Holy Spirit – came *into* the disciples, breaking the sin in their nature, moulding them to holiness, pleading in prayer, and exalting the Saviour.

For reading & meditation – John 20:19-30

A watershed truth

... the grace of the Lord Jesus Christ ... the love of God ... the fellowship of the Holy Spirit ...
2 Corinthians 13:13

*T*he question I have been asked most often about the Trinity is this: Why did not God make clear the truth of the Trinity in the Old Testament and not leave it as something to be deduced in the New Testament? I usually answer like this: Before God could entrust his people with the knowledge of his essential Threeness, he had to lay deep in their minds a piercing conviction of his Oneness. The story of Israel is really the battle of the gods – which god is the real God. Not until belief in one God was laid deep in the consciousness of the Jewish nation was God ready to reveal more clearly to mankind the sublime truth of the Trinity.

For reading & meditation – 2 Corinthians 13:1-14

JANUARY 20

The quality par excellence

Holy, holy, holy is the Lord Almighty ...
Isaiah 6:3

*T*he next aspect of God's nature we examine is that of his *holiness*. What do we mean when we say God is "holy"? There are three thoughts underlying the word "holy". First, the idea of separation, being withdrawn or apart. Second, brightness or brilliance. Third, moral majesty, purity, or cleanliness. It is interesting that those who came into direct contact with the Almighty in the Old Testament were inevitably overwhelmed by his moral majesty. We don't hear much about the holiness of God in today's Church, but then, as now, reverent worship and fear of the Lord is – as the psalmist so beautifully put it – the beginning of wisdom (Psa. 111:10).

For reading & meditation – Isaiah 6:1-13

A prod towards perfection

*... what does the Lord your God ask of
you but to fear the Lord your God ...*
Deuteronomy 10:12

*M*any in today's Church present the love of God
in such a way that it has given rise to the saying
"God loves me as I am." When I have heard people
say this and have questioned them, I have found
the idea in many minds is this: "God loves me as I
am, and whether I go on from here or whether I
stay the same, it makes no difference to his love
for me." That is entirely true, but it is not the en-
tire truth. Because God is love, he loves us as we
are, but because he is *holy* love, he loves us too
much to let us stay as we are.

For reading & meditation – Deuteronomy 10:12-22

JANUARY 22

The fear of God

To fear the Lord is to hate evil ...
Proverbs 8:13

*W*e are taught over and over again in Scripture that because God is uniquely and awesomely holy – pure, separated, and shining in his moral majesty – we are to draw near to him with godly reverence and fear. The fear of the Lord is the beginning of wisdom. There is a fear that helps and a fear that hinders. How do we know the difference? The fear that helps is the fear that expresses itself in reverence, veneration, awe, a sense of the grandeur and majesty of God. The fear that hinders is described for us in 2 Timothy 1:7: "For God did not give us a spirit of timidity but a spirit of power, of love and of self-discipline."

For reading & meditation – Proverbs 8:1-21

J A N U A R Y   23

The power of holiness

*Exalt the Lord our God and wor-
ship at his footstool; he is holy.*
Psalm 99:5

*U*ntil we have been gripped by that nameless
terror which results when an unholy creature is
suddenly confronted by the One who is holiest of
all, we are not likely to be much affected by the
doctrine of love and grace. We will be of little use
to God unless we know how to tremble before him,
for otherwise our own ideas and feelings of self-
sufficiency will soon take over. Have we lost the
sense of awe when we come into God's presence
which seemed to characterise the saints of the past?
I am afraid we have.

For reading & meditation – Psalm 99:1-9

J A N U A R Y   24

Our trustworthy God

... he is the faithful God, keeping his covenant
of love to a thousand generations ...
Deuteronomy 7:9

*W*e move on now to consider another aspect of
God's character – his abiding faithfulness. In an
age when so much unfaithfulness abounds, how
good it is to lift our eyes to the heavens and realize that there we have One who will never let us
down, never have to apologize for failing us, and
never go back on his Word. How refreshing it is,
then, to read today's text and focus our gaze on
the One who is faithful at all times and in all things.
We may let him down but he will never let us down.

For reading & meditation – Deuteronomy 7:7-20

Great is Thy faithfulness

*Your love, O Lord, reaches to the
heavens, your faithfulness to the skies.*
Psalm 36:5

*C*an't you just feel the energy that flows from
the Scriptures buttressing your confidence in God
as you read or hear his Word? For God to be unfaithful would be to act contrary to his nature, and
if he ever was (we are only speculating because
he could never do so) then he would cease to be
God. Everything about God is vast and incompa-
rable, including his faithfulness. He never forgets
a thing, never makes a mistake, never fails to keep
a promise, never falters over a decision, never re-
tracts a statement he has made, and has never
breached a contract.

For reading & meditation – Psalm 36:1-12

JANUARY   26

The need to know

*Let us hold unswervingly to the hope
we profess, for he who promised is faithful.*
Hebrews 10:23

I wish I had the space to take you through the pages of Scripture and show you how faithful God has been to his Word. But you have a Bible for yourself; study it and peruse it. Read it, not merely to know the principles of godliness, but to know God. It is absolutely imperative that we who live in such an age as this, an age when unfaithfulness abounds, should acquaint ourselves with the fact of God's faithfulness. This is the basis of our confidence in him. The more of God's truth we pack into our souls, the better equipped we are for the road that lies ahead.

For reading & meditation – Hebrews 10:19-31

JANUARY 27

"Standing on the promises"

*... he has given us his very
great and precious promises ...*
2 Peter 1:4

*T*here are, nevertheless, literally hundreds of promises God has given us in his Word that we can claim without equivocation. "I will never leave thee, nor forsake thee" (Heb 13:5, AV) is just one among many. Someone who has counted all God's promises in the Bible numbers them as being over 3, 000. That ought to be enough to keep you going if you lived to be a hundred. Be careful, however, that it is a general promise you are banking on, not a specific one.

For reading & meditation – 2 Peter 1:1-11

JANUARY 28

He can't forget!

*Jesus answered, 'The work of God is
this: to believe in the one he has sent.'*
John 6:29

*A*n old saint who was dying became concerned
that he couldn't remember any of God's promises.
His pastor said: "Do you think that God will forget any of them?" A smile came over the face of
the dying Christian as he exclaimed joyfully: "No,
no, he won't." The understanding of this glorious
truth that God is faithful and utterly trustworthy
will deliver us from such incapacitating emotions
as worry, anxiety, and fear. When you think about
it, to be overwhelmed by the concerns of this life
reflects poorly upon the faithfulness of God.

For reading & meditation – John 6:25-33

JANUARY 29

God's wrath

... I will take vengeance on my adversaries and repay those who hate me.
Deuteronomy 32:41

*G*od's *wrath* is a theme about which little is said in today's Church, but though the subject may be missing from many modern-day pulpits, it is not missing from the Bible. If you take hold of a Bible concordance and look up all the texts that refer to the wrath, anger, or the severity of God, you will find that there are more references to these than there are to his love, his graciousness, or his tenderness. Indeed, I would go as far as to say that a proper study of God can never be complete unless consideration is given to the fact that God is not only a God of love but a God of wrath and anger also.

For reading & meditation – Deuteronomy 32:36-47

JANUARY 30

God's great intolerance

... they have rejected the law of the Lord Almighty ... Therefore the Lord's anger burns ...
Isaiah 5:24,25

*T*hose who see God's wrath as petulance or retaliation, inflicting punishment for the sake of it, or in return for some injury received, do not really understand it. Divine wrath is not vindictiveness; it is divine perfection and issues forth from God because it is right. Divine anger must never be confused with human anger. Most of what goes on in our hearts whenever we are angry is a mixture of unpredictable petulance, retaliation, hostility, and self-concern. God's anger is always predictable, always steadfast, and always set against sin.

For reading & meditation – Isaiah 5:18-25

JANUARY 31

FEBRUARY

Righteous indignation

*The wrath of God is being revealed ... against
all the godlessness and wickedness of men ...*
Romans 1:18

*F*or many of us "wrath" conjures up the idea of
being out of control, an outburst of "seeing red",
a sense of wounded pride or just downright
petulance. It is quite wrong to take these ideas or
feelings and impose them on God. God's wrath is
never out of control, never capricious, never self-
indulgent, never irritable, and never ignoble. God
is angry only when anger is called for. Would a
God who took as much pleasure in evil as he did
in good be a God we could love? Would a God
who did not react adversely to evil be morally
perfect? Of course not.

For reading & meditation – Romans 1:8-25

FEBRUARY 1

The unyielding Judge

Settle matters quickly with your adversary who is taking you to court.
Matthew 5:25

"*G*od's wrath," said George MacDonald, "is always *judicial*." It is always the wrath of the Judge administering justice. Those who experience the fullness of God's wrath get precisely what they deserve. That may sound hard, but it is true. Many people live under the illusion that perhaps it might be possible to find a way of escaping all that is required of us in this world. But there is no such escape. A way to avoid the demands of righteousness, apart from the righteousness which God accounts to us at the cross, would not be moral.

For reading & meditation – Matthew 5:21-26

FEBRUARY 2

Heaven or hell

In hell, where he was in torment, he looked
up and saw Abraham far away ...
Luke 16:23

*T*he final state of those who die without availing themselves of the forgiveness God offers them at the Cross is eternal banishment from God's presence. The Bible calls this "hell". "There is no heaven with a little hell in it," said George MacDonald, meaning that the God who is passionately for righteousness and implacably against sin must ensure that the two are finally separated. However, hell is always something that people choose for themselves. It is a state for which men and women opt. God says to those who die impenitent: "You preferred your own way to mine; you shall have it – for ever."

For reading & meditation – Luke 16:19-31

FEBRUARY 3

~❦~

Love with a 'stoop'

*Let us then approach the throne
of grace with confidence ...*
Hebrews 4:16

*W*e turn now to consider an aspect of God's nature which on the surface seems so close to love that many regard it as simply a synonym for it. I refer to that facet of God's character which we describe as "grace". I heard an old Welsh preacher say this: "Grace is a word with a 'stoop' in it; love reaches out on the same level, but grace always has to stoop to pick one up. Grace then is God's kindness bestowed upon the undeserving; benevolence handed down to those who have no merit; a hand reaching down to those who have fallen into a pit. The Bible bids us believe that on the throne of the universe there is a God like that.

For reading & meditation – Hebrews 4:1-16

FEBRUARY 4

Amazing!

*So too, at the present time there is
a remnant chosen by grace.*
Romans 11:5

It must be understood right away that grace is a characteristic of God which is exercised only toward those who are seen as having a special relationship with him – those God foreknew would be brought into a special relationship with himself through his Son, Jesus Christ. Arthur W. Pink says: "Grace is the sole source from which flows the goodwill, love and salvation of God into his *chosen* people." Grace cannot be bought, earned, deserved, or merited. If it could, it would cease to be grace. Grace flows down as pure charity, "falling on the unloveable and making it lovely". Amazing!

For reading & meditation – Romans 11:1-24

FEBRUARY 5

Sovereign grace

For it is by grace you have been saved,
through faith ... it is the gift of God ...
Ephesians 2:8

*T*he old definition of grace which almost every
Christian will know is one that I believe cannot be
improved: "Grace is the free unmerited favour of
God." It means that at the heart of all true com-
munion with God there lies this gripping truth –
God took the initiative. He is more inclined towards us than we are towards him. We cannot earn
his affection any more than we can earn a loving
mother's affection. Grace is a gift. You have not to
achieve but simply receive.

For reading & meditation – Ephesians 2:1-10

FEBRUARY 6

We've won a holiday

In him we have ... the forgiveness of sins, in
accordance with the riches of God's grace ...
Ephesians 1:7

*H*ow can Christ's righteousness be imputed and
imparted to us? It's *his* righteousness, not ours. A
simple illustration may help to illuminate this
point. A dull little boy came home from school
one day and said to his mother: "*We've* won a holiday." The truth was another boy had come top of
the region in the examinations and the head teacher
decided to give the whole school a holiday. Yet the
dull little lad said: "We've won a holiday." Grace
is like that. God permits the righteousness of Jesus
to cover us and then, as we open ourselves to it –
to enter us. *He* did it, but *we* benefit from it. Isn't
grace *really* amazing?

For reading & meditation – Ephesians 1:1-14

FEBRUARY 7

The God of all grace

But by the grace of God I am what I am ...
1 Corinthians 15:10

I sense that the Church once again is in danger of losing out to legalism as more and more Christians get caught up with *doing* rather than *being*. Talk to people about what they are doing and they are with you at once; talk to them about being (who they really are) and their attitude is one of deferential blankness. The Church of Jesus Christ is in a sad state when it can't say with conviction and meaning, as did the apostle Paul: "By the grace of God I am what I am."

For reading & meditation – 1 Corinthians 15:1-11

God knows all

... I know what is going through your mind.
Ezekiel 11:5

*T*he final aspect of God's nature that we examine is his knowledge and wisdom. The difference between knowledge and wisdom has been described like this: "Knowledge is what we know; wisdom is the right application of what we know." God, of course, knows everything; everything possible, everything actual. He is perfectly acquainted with every detail in the life of every being in heaven, in earth, and in hell. Nothing escapes his notice, nothing can be hidden from him, and nothing can be forgotten by him.

For reading & meditation – Ezekiel 11:1-15

FEBRUARY 9

Reflect on perfection

They will speak of the glorious splendour of your majesty, and I will meditate on your wonderful works.
Psalm 145:5

*T*he fact that God knows everything ought to strengthen our faith and cause us to bow in adoration before him. To the believer, the truth of God's omniscience (all knowledge) ought to be one of tremendous comfort and security. In times of perplexity we ought to say like Job: "He knows the way that I take; when he has tested me, I shall come forth as gold" (Job 23:10). Whatever might be going on in our lives that is profoundly mysterious to us and quite incomprehensible to those who are around us, we must never lose sight of the fact that "he knows the way that [we] take".

For reading & meditation – Psalm 145:1-20

FEBRUARY 10

The God who sees

"... I have now seen the One who sees me."
Genesis 16:13

*W*hat matters most – that I know God or that God knows me? I think the latter. I am graven on the palms of his hands. I am never out of his thoughts. It was this that Hagar came to see when she was feeling utterly bereft and forgotten – that God saw her and knew everything there was to know about her. "I have now seen the One who sees me," she said. There is unspeakable comfort in knowing that God knows all about us. I don't think we have quite got hold of this truth in modern times as it is something that is rarely preached or written about.

For reading & meditation – Genesis 16:1-16

FEBRUARY 11

Fullness – only in God

*... to the only wise God be glory
for ever through Jesus Christ!*
Romans 16:27

I remember speaking to a Christian youth group once on the subject of God's wisdom, and before I began I asked if someone could offer a suggested definition of the subject under discussion. One young man said: "God's wisdom is the ability to get us through scrapes and difficulties without getting hurt." I gave the young man full marks for attempting a definition, but I had to show him that was not what divine wisdom is all about. The goal behind divine wisdom is not to make us happy but to make us holy.

For reading & meditation – Romans 16:17-27

FEBRUARY 12

God's one great goal

*For those God foreknew he also predestined to be
conformed to the likeness of his Son ...*
Romans 8:29

*T*hose who think that God's wisdom is engaged
in endeavouring to get them through life without
having to face personal discomfort or pain have
no real understanding of this divine attribute. What
is God's great goal in the universe to which his
energies are devoted? We have it in our text for
today. God's great energy and wisdom, working
on behalf of all Christians, is directed to making
us like his Son Jesus Christ. Of course this purpose will only be fully realized in the world to
come, but while we are here he is pursuing that
selfsame purpose nevertheless.

For reading & meditation – Romans 8:28-39

FEBRUARY 13

Some extra practice

Consider it pure joy, my brothers,
whenever you face trials of many kinds ...
James 1:2

*W*e should never be taken aback when unexpected and upsetting things happen to us. Our first reaction should be to recognize that no matter how hard the trial, God's power will be there to get us through, and God's wisdom will ensure that the trial will be worth more than it costs. I like the almost tongue-in-cheek way Jim Packer describes what may be God's point of view when he permits us to go through trials: "Perhaps he means to strengthen us in patience, good humour, compassion, humility, or meekness by giving us some extra practice in exercising these graces under specially difficult situations."

For reading & meditation – James 1:1-18

FEBRUARY   14

~·//·~

Our only hope

> *... I am the Lord, who exercises kindness,*
> *justice and righteousness on earth ...*
> Jeremiah 9:24

*I*t's interesting isn't it, as our passage for today shows, that when the Lord talks about himself in the Scriptures it is usually in terms of his attributes or character traits: kindness, justice, righteousness, and so on. And there is a clear and definite purpose in this: the more we know of God the more established our lives will be here on the earth. That kind of God-understanding and God-awareness is our only hope for coping with twenty-first century problems.

For reading & meditation – Jeremiah 9:17-24

FEBRUARY 15

The truth in a nutshell

*... the people who know their
God will firmly resist him.*
Daniel 11:32

*T*he most natural thing in the world when there is
a good relationship between parents and their child
is for that child to want to become like them. That
is the way it is also with God our Father. The more
we discover of his love, his holiness, his purity,
his trustworthiness, his strength, his patience, the
more we want to emulate him. You can only know
God, of course, through Christ, and because you
have him, instead of saying, "Look what the world
has come to," you will be able to say: "Look what
has come to the world."

For reading & meditation – Daniel 11:14-35

FEBRUARY 16

When God laughs

The One enthroned in heaven
laughs; the Lord scoffs at them.
Psalm 2:4

*S*ometimes we get depressed as we look at the state of the world and see the Church derided and discarded by the men and women of this age. The psalm before us today reminds us that at any moment God can arise and confound his enemies: "The One enthroned in heaven laughs." Why *laughs*? Because as he sees the little people of this earth strutting so arrogantly through all their days, he knows that at a word he can destroy them all. He could do it, but he won't, for divine purposes are being worked out. How different life would be if we could learn to look at it through God's eyes rather than our own.

For reading & meditation – Psalm 2:1-12

FEBRUARY 17

The greatest sin

*But you did not honour the God who holds
in his hand your life and all your ways.*
Daniel 5:23

*W*hy do respectable people who come into our churches have a struggle to believe they are sinners? Because they are under the impression that sin consists in vices such as drunkenness, adultery, dishonesty, and so on. They haven't committed any of these evils so they do not think of themselves as "sinners". But the essence of sin is the *failure to glorify God*, and anyone who does not glorify God is guilty of the worst kind of sin. What makes them sinners is *living for themselves and their own glory*.

For reading & meditation – Daniel 5:17-31

FEBRUARY 18

Surprises – easy to miss

He made known his ways to Moses,
his deeds to the people of Israel.
Psalm 103:7

*I*t is so easy to go through life missing God's surprises because we don't know how to spot them, or, conversely, to "spiritualize" ordinary events and read into them more than we should. Sometimes God's surprises explode in our lives like firecrackers; at other times we squint into the forest wondering if what we see really is an albino or just an abandoned washing machine. Every one of us needs to understand the reasons why God delights to surprise us. Then we shall be less likely to miss them – or misinterpret them.

For reading & meditation – Psalm 103:1-22

FEBRUARY 19

Glory in the commonplace

How awesome is this place!
This is ... the house of God ...
Genesis 28:17

*G*od surprises us by revealing himself to us at the most unexpected times and in the most unexpected places. God's favoured way of meeting his children is, of course, around his Word, the Bible, but this does not mean he will meet us only there. He does not wait for what we might call the "grand moments" of life. Sometimes he surprises us by making the commonplace grand. Galilee and Glasgow are just the same to him.

For reading & meditation – Genesis 28:1-22

FEBRUARY 20

Crammed with heaven

*So Moses thought, "I will go over
and see this strange sight ..."*
Exodus 3:3

I must confess that in the early days of my Christian life the idea of God revealing himself through the ordinary was a most surprising one to me. However, we must not overlook the fact that God sometimes surprises us by coming to us in the most unexpected ways and places. It is possible to walk about blind to the glory that is around us because we do not expect to find it there. Therefore we need the discerning eye – the power to see the glory in the ordinary, to walk down familiar pathways and see unfamiliar things.

For reading & meditation – Exodus 3:1-15

FEBRUARY 21

A muffled cry

*For I was hungry and you gave
me something to eat ...*
Matthew 25:35

A missionary couple found a woman with an infant in her arms. The woman told them that she was unable to have children and her prayer had been that God would give her a child. One day, a few weeks past, she had been returning home when she found an abandoned baby. Had God answered her prayer? Taking the child first to the police to certify that it had been abandoned, she asked to keep it. They agreed, so cleaned and warm, the child slept peacefully in her arms. That muffled cry she believes (and so do I) was the faint reminder that the Spirit of the living Christ is everywhere.

For reading & meditation – Matthew 25:31-46

F E B R U A R Y   22

Reach out – now

When he looks at me, he sees the one who sent me.
John 12:45

I feel it will be helpful to spend another day meditating on the ordinariness of Jesus. It was because he mingled the commonplace with the glorious, and came along a frequented path, that so few were able to recognize him. The unusual and the ostentatious are always more attractive than the truly great and the truly grand. A preacher tells how one evening he stood with a group of friends as a firework display was just about to begin. While he waited, he turned and saw behind him an exceptionally glorious sunset. Excited, he exclaimed: "Look at that!" But no one looked – they were too engrossed in watching a man lighting a common squib.

For reading & meditation – John 12:37-50

FEBRUARY 23

Job's bar exam

*Brace yourself like a man; I will
question you, and you shall answer me.*
Job 38:3

Job declared in chapter 23:3-7: "If only I knew
where to find him ..." God turns the tables on Job
by asking *him* some searching questions. "Where
were you when I laid the earth's foundations? Who
marked off its dimensions? Who stretched a
measuring line across it?" One after the other the
questions came. Job became nonplussed but
eventually got the point: there were some things he
would never understand, and because God is who
he is, he should be taken on trust. Job didn't have
his questions answered but he did see God. That
was enough.

For reading & meditation – Job 38:1-18

F E B R U A R Y   24

Everything – for the best

> *... great is your faithfulness. I say to*
> *myself, "The Lord is my portion ..."*
> Lamentations 3:24

*Y*esterday we examined Job's attempt to get God
to give him some clear answers to the perplexities
that had troubled him. We saw that instead of
answers he gained a greater awareness of God. He
came to see that God was perfectly capable of running his world, and deserved to be taken on trust.
Sometimes I wonder if trying to interpret the ways
of God to people becomes counter-productive.
Perhaps there is more solace in simply recognising
that God is bigger than we are and that we can
trust him to work out everything for the best.

For reading & meditation – Lamentations 3:1-26

Pain – God's megaphone

*Three times I pleaded with the Lord to
take [a thorn in my flesh] away from me.*
2 Corinthians 12:8

*G*od's people down the running ages have discovered that surprising things happen to them in times of great difficulty and pain. C.S. Lewis's famous statement brings the truth fully into focus: "Pain is God's megaphone to rouse a deaf world." He made the point also that God's primary concern is not that we be happy, but that we be holy. When Lewis talked about pain he was not thinking only of physical pain, but of spiritual and psychological pain also. Sometimes this is the only way God can get our attention; pain becomes his "megaphone" to rouse our inattentive and sleepy spirits.

For reading & meditation – 2 Corinthians 12:1-10

FEBRUARY 26

Our "terrible freedom"

> *... I have come that they may*
> *have life, and have it to the full.*
> John 10:10

*I*t's strange how we view God as a killjoy when really he is a "filljoy". Obviously, that is not his fault but ours. Our text for today tells us he gives life, and that more abundantly. Why then do we not believe it? Why are we so surprised when, having surrendered to him, we find his words to be true? One reason, I think, is because to hold on to the concept of God as a killjoy makes it easier to justify our unwillingness to surrender to his claims. Of course, refusing to surrender is our freedom. As C.S. Lewis put it, it is "a *terrible* freedom".

For reading & meditation – John 10:1-10

The last word

"To whom will you compare me? Or who is my equal?" says the Holy One.
Isaiah 40:25

*G*od's work is seen clearly "only now and then". The Almighty breaks into the world and into lives with surprises that serve as mountain peaks from which we can view the rest of his more subtle work. I wonder how many surprises the Lord has waiting for you in the year that lies ahead. Learn to look out for them; for you never know what God is going to do next. One can go through the woods or through a whole year missing elusive surprises – sunsets, deer, brooks, birds, and strange stirrings in our lives.

For reading & meditation – Isaiah 40:18-31

FEBRUARY 28

Feelings can be liars!

*The tribes go up ... to praise the name of the
Lord according to the statute given to Israel.*
Psalm 122:4-5

*T*he Biblical position is this: whether or not we
feel like it, we should instruct our souls to worship the Lord. Feelings very often are liars. If I
worshipped only when I felt like it then my life
would be fairly devoid of worship. "Worship is an
act which develops feelings for God, not a feeling
for God which is expressed in an act of worship."
When we obey the command to worship God and
offer him our worship even though we do not feel
like it then something happens in our souls that is
quite amazing.

For reading & meditation – Psalm 122:1-9

MARCH

Are you willing?

I do believe; help me overcome my unbelief!
Mark 9:24

You may be caught up in the midst of some personal tragedy at this very moment and feel as if you are being sucked down into a whirlpool of despair. "Now is the time for one of God's great surprises," you may be saying to yourself. "If he is loving as he says he is, then why doesn't he do something? Why?" The best position to take in times of trouble is the position of trust. The principle is this – when fullness of trust is difficult, first identify the fact that you already have some trust, then ask for more. You will receive from God only as much as you are *willing* to receive.

For reading & meditation – Mark 9:14-32

MARCH 1

Doing what the Father does

... whatever the Father does the Son also does.
John 5:19

*L*ife on this sin-cursed planet is a struggle and sometimes a strain. There are some, I know, who will say: "Come on now, let's not be too pessimistic. Life can be bad but it can also be a ball." We should ask our Father in heaven what to pray for and how to pray. In the passage before us we see Jesus healing just one out of a whole group of needy people. Why only one? As our text tells us, he looked first to heaven to see what his Father was doing and then he joined hands in ministering towards that self-same end.

For reading & meditation – John 5:1-23

MARCH 2

Not the answer we expect

*You still lack one thing. Sell everything
you have ... Then come, follow me.*
Luke 18:22

*T*oday we examine the attitude of the rich young
ruler who said to Jesus: "Good teacher, what must
I do to inherit eternal life?" (v. 18). Our Lord's
reply was clear and to the point: "Sell everything
you have and give to the poor, and you will have
treasure in heaven. Then come, follow me". But
the young man loved his wealth more than he loved
God. That was why Jesus condemned it. Our Lord
is not against people having wealth; he is only
against them making wealth their god.

For reading & meditation – Luke 18:18-30

MARCH 3

No place for idols

Dear children, keep yourselves from idols.
1 John 5:21

I believe John knew the tendency in all our hearts towards divided loyalty. We usually associate idols with a low-level expression of religion – the idols of pagan faiths. But idols are an expression of a universal tendency – the tendency to substitute something in the place of God. Idolatry is a substitution – the substitution of the lesser for the greater. There is nothing worse than Christian idolatry, that is when we don't go as far as to reject God; we simply put something else at the centre and God is then marginalised. There he can only faintly influence our lives – and the result is weakness and immaturity.

For reading & meditation – 1 John 5:1-21

MARCH 4

That one dear face

The Son is the radiance of God's glory
and the exact representation of his being ...
Hebrews 1:3

*I*s Jesus an idol, coming between us and God?
An idol misrepresents God; Jesus represents him.
Is Jesus like God in status, character and life? Fully
and truly like him? I would respond with an un-
qualified "Yes". Jesus fulfils the chief desire
behind most forms of idolatry – to have God near
and understandable. We have in Jesus a God with
a face. "Is your face towards me Daddy?" said a
little boy to his father, who had taken his son into
his own bed because he was afraid of a midnight
storm. "Yes," replied the father, "it is." The little
boy then soon fell asleep. Jesus gives God a face
and that face is towards us – always.

For reading & meditation – Hebrews 1:1-14

M A R C H   5

A secret of success

When he had received the drink,
Jesus said, "It is finished."
John 19:30

*T*here were many things the disciples (and others) wanted our Lord to do which he steadfastly resisted. And he did so because his main concern was to follow his Father's agenda, not the agenda of others. Is not this the secret of spiritual success? One of the reasons why we get spiritually run down, anaemic, and out of sorts is because we spend our lives responding to what others want us to do rather than finding out what God wants us to do – and sticking to it. Our Lord glorified the Father because he got his job description directly from the Father's hand and not from the hands of others. So must we.

For reading & meditation – John 19:28-37

MARCH 6

Out of the world

*... you do not belong to the world, but
I have chosen you out of the world ...*
John 15:19

A disciple of Christ is someone who does not
belong to this world. This might seem a small point
to many but it is something that is written into the
very warp and woof of Scripture. If we are of the
world we are not of Christ, and if we are of Christ
we are not of the world. I know we open ourselves
to criticism from non-Christians when we say we
are not of the world. They condemn us for putting
ourselves in a separate compartment. But this is
what salvation is all about – being in the world
but not of it.

For reading & meditation – John 15:18-27

MARCH 7

A Great High Priest

For we do not have a high priest who is unable to sympathize with our weaknesses ...
Hebrews 4:15

*T*he disciples could not always understand the master but they stayed with him through thick and thin. To "obey the Word" does not mean we will never have times of doubt and struggle, but that we hold on to it nevertheless. The true disciples of Jesus realize that nothing matters in this world more than the truth of God, and even in the midst of their struggles they allow themselves to be dominated and controlled by that truth. He keeps us and we keep his Word.

For reading & meditation – Hebrews 5:1-16

M A R C H   8

My joy!

*Ask and you will receive, and
your joy will be complete.*
John 16:24

*S*ome think that joy is a matter of temperament.
But the joy our Lord longs for his disciples to pos-
sess has nothing to do with temperament, it is a
joy that comes directly from him. "My joy." This
joy does not depend on physical or psychological
conditions. It is not self-generated – we cannot
reach down into the depths of our being and pump
it up. Christ possesses it in all its fullness, and
when we live in him, he then gives it to us. It is as
simple as that. Permit me to ask the question: Do
you have this kind of joy?

For reading & meditation – John 16:17-24

MARCH 9

A little bit of heaven!

... yet I will rejoice in the Lord,
I will be joyful in God my Saviour.
Habakkuk 3:18

*W*e cannot have heaven in all its fullness now, and Christian history shows that the prospect of one day arriving at a place where everything is perfect and complete has served to nerve many a weary traveller forward. Of this there can be no doubt. But unless we are careful and get the balance right we will lose out on the fact that although we cannot get heaven here on earth, we can get a little bit of heaven to go to heaven in. To put it bluntly, we are fools if we think that we cannot get something of the joys of heaven in the here and now.

For reading & meditation – Habakkuk 3:1-19

M A R C H   10

Hated by the world

*Do not conform any longer
to the pattern of this world ...*
Romans 12:2

*W*e can't get very far in the Christian life unless
we remember that we and the world are going in
different directions. Another fact that we must not
fail to recognize is that once we come over on to
the side of Christ then the world hates us. Does
the world hate us as it hated our Lord? I doubt it –
at least not here in the West. The world did not
hate Jesus because he was deliberately antagonis-
tic. It hated him because of his sheer purity and
holiness. It will be the same with us.

For reading & meditation – Romans 12:1-8

MARCH 11

Why Christians are hated

Do not be surprised, my brothers,
if the world hates you.
1 John 3:13

*T*he world hates the true Christian because Christ himself and the true Christian condemn the natural man in a way that nobody else does. In a strange way non-Christians detect in a Christian that he or she is not depending on their own strength and ability but on the strength and ability of Another – and that runs counter to their pride. The ultimate problem with the human heart is that of pride, and this is why the most moral people are the ones who so often hate Christ most of all. And those who are unwilling to give up their pride cannot stand such condemnation. So they hate the true Christian as they hated Christ.

For reading & meditation – 1 John 3:11-24

MARCH 12

Influence or intelligence?

*Your enemy the devil prowls around like a roaring
lion looking for someone to devour.*
1 Peter 5:8

I sometimes meet Christians who tell me they
don't believe in a personal devil and my response
is usually this: "You may not believe in the devil
but I assure you – the devil believes in you." Satan
has a great variety of strategies which he uses to
attack Christ's disciples, but his chief weapon is
the one he used in Eden and which, as we know,
proved so successful – *doubt*. Doubt is not an evil
in itself, but when allowed to linger and not firmly
ejected it can soon lead to a loss of confidence in
God.

For reading & meditation – 1 Peter 5:1-14

MARCH 13

Inner health

I rejoiced with those who said to me,
"Let us go to the house of the Lord."
Psalm 122:1

C.S. Lewis realised that it is through worship that God communicates his presence to us. The essence of the Jewish sacrifices, he pointed out, was that when men and women gave bulls and goats to God, he gave himself to them. God is thinking more of us than himself when he bids us worship him. For it is in the worship of him that we complete ourselves. Our souls find their highest potential as we pour out our hearts in worship and adoration. Perhaps this is what C.S. Lewis had in mind when he said: "Worship is inner health made audible."

For reading & meditation – Psalm 122:1-9

MARCH 14

Calloused hearts

*... if we hold firmly till the end
the confidence we had at first.*
Hebrews 3:14

*T*he failure of the children of Israel to enter into the Promised Land the first time they arrived at its borders is one of the great tragedies of the Old Testament. When they came to the borders of Canaan and could have entered into its rest, they drew back in fear. This condition is labelled by the writer of Hebrews as having an "unbelieving heart". Unbelief kept a whole nation out of the Promised Land, and it will keep us out of spiritual blessing too. If the Israelites were excluded because they did not listen to Moses, how much more will we be excluded if we do not listen to the Son.

For reading & meditation – Hebrews 3:12-19

MARCH 15

It's action that's needed

... those who heard did not combine it with faith.
Hebrews 4:2

*F*aith is more than mere belief, faith is *acting* upon that belief. The old theologians used to say that faith has three components: knowledge, self-committal, and trust. All three have to be in operation for faith to reach its goal. The goal of all that God wants to do for us on this earth is to bring us from a life of spiritual striving to rest and confidence in him. Note the core problem with which the Israelites constantly struggled: "those who heard did not combine it with faith." In other words, they heard the good tidings but they did not act upon the message.

For reading & meditation – Hebrews 4:1-2

MARCH 16

Entering into God's rest

So I declared on oath in my anger,
"They shall never enter my rest."
Hebrews 4:3

*T*he climax of Israel's rebellion came when they faithlessly refused to undertake the conquest of Canaan and considered returning to Egypt. At that point God withdrew his blessing from them, and barred them from entering into the rest of which he had previously spoken. They were not barred from entering the land, but they were barred from the promised rest. When eventually the Israelites arrived in the land, their rest was interrupted time and time again by marauding armies and fierce battles. The point was being made – the rest of God is only for those who adopt the attitude of perfect trust.

For reading & meditation – Hebrews 4:30

M A R C H   17

Intimate relationships

Blessed is the man whose quiver is full of them. They will not be put to shame ...
Psalm 127:5

*T*he family is the basic unit of society – a divinely intended source of comfort. Life is really all about relationships – our relationship with God and relationships with others. Respect for people must be at the centre of all our work if we are Christians. Eugene Peterson said: "The character of our work is shaped not by accomplishments or possessions but in the birth of relationships ... Among those around us we develop sons and daughters, brothers and sisters even as our Lord did with us." Making money is part of work, but developing relationships is part of it too. Happy are those who have their "quivers" full of them.

For reading & meditation – Psalm 127:5

MARCH   18

Of its own accord

*When the Lord brought back the captives
to Zion, we were like men who dreamed.*
Psalm 126:1

*S*amuel Butler said: "All the animals, excepting
man, know the principal business of life is to enjoy it." Pleasure and Christian joy cannot be
equated. Pleasure depends on circumstances. Pleasures come and go. The joy of God is constant. It
rises to rise again. Pleasures are superficial. Joy is
deep. It wells up from inner contentment. The
smile is not merely on the lips and in the eyes but
in the heart. It may flame into rapture or sink into
peace. We don't have to acquire joy. It comes to us
when we experience salvation, of its own accord.

For reading & meditation – Psalm 126:1-6

MARCH 19

Greater than Joshua

For if Joshua had given them rest, God would
not have spoken later about another day.
Hebrews 4:8

*M*oses led the Israelites out of slavery, yet no
one could lead them into rest – not even Joshua.
Although Joshua was a brilliant military commander, it was beyond his ability to lead the children of Israel into the rest which God had planned
for them because they had disqualified themselves
by their unwillingness to believe. The writer picks
up on the point that a greater than Joshua is here.
The Son not only leads us out of slavery but on
into the Sabbath rest. Only Jesus can say with the
authority of heaven behind him: "Come to me ...
and I will give you rest." (Matt. 11:28).

For reading & meditation – Hebrews 4:6-10

MARCH   20

Arrested development

Anyone who lives on milk ... is not acquainted
with the teaching about righteousness.
Hebrews 5:13

*O*ne of the greatest marks of maturity, is the
ability to distinguish good from evil. Does this mean
we can have decades of Christian experience behind
us and still be immature? I'm afraid it does. No
matter how eloquently we can talk about our faith,
if we can't distinguish good from evil, right from
wrong, we are immature – period. A mistake many
Christians make is to assume that age produces
maturity. It doesn't. Can the same thing be said of
you and me? It's a sobering thought that we may
have been Christians for years and yet be suffering
from arrested spiritual development.

For reading & meditation – Hebrews 5:11-14

MARCH 21

Baby talk!

Therefore let us leave the elementary teachings about Christ and go on to maturity ...
Hebrews 6:1

*T*he three things described as "elementary teachings" are first, the initial act of repentance, second, Church ordinances, and third, eschatology (the things concerning the future). When we talk about these elementary things and nothing else then we are simply indulging in "baby talk". It's time we were weaned on to some solid food. We must not forget, however, that the low level of Christian understanding is directly related to the low level of Christian preaching. If we have problems in the pulpit we should not be surprised if we have problems in the pews.

For reading & meditation – Hebrews 5:14 - 6:2

MARCH 22

Wills that become set

And God permitting, we will do so.
Hebrews 6:3

*T*hese words imply that some will not be able to move on towards maturity because, by their continued desire to remain at their present level, their wills become set in the state of non-growth. This is what someone has described as "the danger of prolonged immaturity" – of remaining in one place so long that we don't want to move on. It is perilously possible to remain so contented with immaturity that the call to maturity leaves us unmoved. If we don't set our wills in the direction of moving ahead with Christ then they can become inflexibly set in the alternative state – the state of non-growth.

For reading & meditation – Hebrews 6:3-6

MARCH 23

Am I really growing?

*... show this same diligence to the very
end, in order to make your hope sure.*
Hebrews 6:11

*A*lthough the writer has faced the Hebrew
Christians with some strong and serious issues,
he follows them up with the encouraging and
hope-building words of our text today. As the writer
thinks of the people to whom he was writing, he is
concerned that they manifest an earnest and
fervent desire to move on in their relationship with
God. Diligence and perseverance is the hallmark
of a successful Christian life and is the proven
pattern for victory.

For reading & meditation – Hebrews 6:9-12

MARCH   24

Thinking Christianly

*Do not conform any longer to the
pattern of this world, but be transformed
by the renewing of your mind.*
Romans 12:2

*T*he Christian Church has always stood in danger
of being brainwashed by the world, but perhaps
never as much as at this present time. Secularism
has spread its tentacles far and wide so that almost
without realising it we find ourselves thinking about
the important issues of life with much the same
mindset as the world. J.B. Phillips translates our
text for today in this way: "Don't let the world
around you squeeze you into its own mould, but let
God remould your minds from within."

For reading & meditation – Romans 12:1-21

The divine exchange

> *But we have the mind of Christ.*
> 1 Corinthians 2:16

*D*uring my early schooldays I was not a very bright student, but after becoming a Christian in my teens I began to comprehend things in a completely different way. My pastor told me: "This is because Christ is now in your mind. You can think best when he is in it." Paul tells the Corinthians in the text before us today that they have the "mind of Christ". Our sovereign Lord places at the disposal of all his children his pure and perfect mind. He opens his mind to us; we must open our minds to him.

For reading & meditation – 1 Corinthians 2:1-16

Wholesome thinking

*I have written ... reminders to stimulate
you to wholesome thinking.*
2 Peter 3:1

*H*ow much of Christ's thinking do we see in the minds of Christians today as they approach the different issues of life? Generally speaking, we seem to give more credence to the ideas of the world than the words of our Lord. When I see how the ideas of the world are dominating the field of Christianity I am deeply saddened. It is not so much that the ideas of the world are never good – at times they are. It is that they come out of a system where Satan reigns. Therefore they must be carefully scrutinized and compared with the Word of God before being accepted and adopted.

For reading & meditation – 2 Peter 3:1-18

MARCH 27

What's it all about?

*... they are zealous for God, but their
zeal is not based on knowledge.*
Romans 10:2

*W*hat Paul wrote about unbelieving Jews in this passage could be said of some modern-day Christians. They have plenty of zeal but not much knowledge. This is because they pay more attention to the things that stir their feelings than the things which inform their minds. Enthusiasm without enlightenment – that sums up the condition of many. Now let no one think that I am in any way playing down feelings and playing up thinking. I am pleading for an equal and balanced concern for both.

For reading & meditation – Romans 10:1-15

MARCH 28

The Master's yoke

Take my yoke upon you and learn from me, for I am gentle and humble in heart ...
Matthew 11:29

*C*hrist likens himself to a farmer and us to oxen in his service. But unlike a farmer who imposes a yoke upon the oxen whether they like it or not, Christ invites us to carry his yoke. "Take my yoke upon you." The difficulty all educationalists face is getting their pupils to give their minds to them in the same way that they give their minds to their pupils. Christ gives his mind to us, but are we willing to give our minds to him? One thing is sure – if Christ doesn't have our minds then he doesn't have us. For as a man thinks, so is he.

For reading & meditation – Matthew 11:20-30

MARCH   29

Two different burdens

This is love for God: to obey his commands.
And his commands are not burdensome.
1 John 5:3

*W*hen Christ calls those who are "weary and burdened" to come to him, he is summoning those who are weighed down with sin and guilt. The difference between the two burdens is this: the burden of sinfulness is difficult and heavy; the burden of service is easy and light. The reason why God's commands are not burdensome is because to love is what our souls were made for, and when we fulfil the command to love we fulfil ourselves. The highest characteristic in God – love – is also the highest characteristic in us.

For reading & meditation – 1 John 5:1-12

Change your mind

*"You do not want to leave too,
do you?" Jesus asked the Twelve.*
John 6:67

*O*ne significant fact that is apparent from the Gospels is this – the early disciples willingly put their minds under the tutelage of Christ. Their understanding of truth was shaped and moulded by the teachings of Jesus. Sometimes they were shocked by our Lord's words and attitudes and appear to have been reconsidering their commitment to him. Have you not had similar moments in your own pilgrimage with Christ? Our Lord's teachings flow from a mind that is incarnate wisdom. He is right in everything.

For reading & meditation – John 6:53-69

MARCH 31

APRIL

God's powerful laser

*The man without the Spirit does not accept
the things that come from the Spirit of God ...*
1 Corinthians 2:14

*W*ho has not experienced times when their own
thinking and Christ's thinking seem to lead in
opposite directions? Why should this be? Largely
it is due to the effects that Adam and Eve's
original sin have had upon the human personality.
Everywhere in the Bible the mind is seen as
having been deeply affected by the Fall. The
person without the Spirit sees the truth of God as
foolishness. That is why unless the Holy Spirit
assists a person to come to Christ, he or she will
never be able to enter into his kingdom. Only
Christ saves; no one can save himself or herself.

For reading & meditation – 1 Corinthians 2:1-16

APRIL 1

Our thinking vs God's

For the message of the cross is foolishness
to those who are perishing ...
1 Corinthians 1:18

*W*e tend to think that the way to independence is by getting out from under authority. God says differently: "Everyone must submit himself to the governing authorities" (Rom. 13:1). We tend to think the way to get ahead is by covering up our mistakes. God says the opposite: "He who conceals his sins does not prosper, but whoever confesses and renounces them finds mercy" (Prov. 28:13). We tend to think that if we surrender our lives to God we will lose them. Jesus said: "Whoever loses his life for me will find it." (Matt. 10:39)

For reading & meditation – 1 Corinthians 1:10-31

APRIL 2

Two stages of education

*But the Counsellor ... will teach you all
things and will remind you of everything ...*
John 14:26

*T*he disciples' learning was a gradual process
which began when Christ's earthly presence was
with them, and continued with the descent of the
Holy Spirit at Pentecost. In so many matters they
had to choose between the current Jewish beliefs
and the wisdom of Christ and the Holy Spirit. And
make no mistake about it, the two were often in
direct conflict. But the disciples were determined
to bring their minds, and the minds of those to
whom they ministered, under the authority and
continued tutelage of Christ.

For reading & meditation – John 14:15-31

APRIL 3

The basis of humility

When I consider ... the work of your fingers ...
what is man that you are mindful of him ...?
Psalm 8:3-4

I feel that the people of the world do not really understand *humility*. In Christian tradition, humility ranks high. Chrysostom, one of the Church Fathers, believed: "Humility is the foundation of our philosophy." Augustine said: "If you ask me what is the first precept of the Christian religion I will answer, first, second, and third, humility." Such appreciation of humility springs from the conviction expressed by the psalmist in today's passage that mankind is made from the dust, and is totally dependent on God for existence and survival.

For reading & meditation – Psalm 8:1-9

APRIL 4

True success

Before his downfall a man's heart is proud,
but humility comes before honour.
Proverbs 18:12

*S*ome confuse humility with an inferiority complex. True humility does not come out of a complex; it comes out of Christ. It is not the result of being mishandled in childhood but the consequence of intimate fellowship with a loving heavenly Father, and of viewing oneself against the backdrop of his everlasting mercy and love. Others confuse humility with lack of ambition. The truly humble are the most ambitious souls alive, but they are ambitious about the right things and for the right reasons.

For reading & meditation – Proverbs 18:1-15

APRIL 5

The seed-bed of humility

Do not think of yourself more highly than you ought,
but rather think of yourself with sober judgment ...
Romans 12:3

The best definition of humility the secular mind can offer is "Humble – having or showing low estimate of one's own importance." Now compare that with Paul's understanding of humility, as given in our text for today. He tells us not to have an exaggerated opinion of our own importance, but to think about ourselves with sober judgment. Humility, then, is a conscious and realistic appraisal of oneself – an appraisal made in the context of God and his grace. Pride grows out of a wrong comparison and humility grows out of a right comparison.

For reading & meditation – Romans 12:1-8

APRIL 6

Look up!

*I lift up my eyes to the hills –
where does my help come from?*
Psalm 121:1

*W*hen we lose touch with God – the true God –
we lose touch with ourselves and we lose touch
with the source of humility. This turns the definitions of many concerning humility on their head
– definitions such as this one which I came across
in my reading the other day: "Humility never looks
up, or out, but always down." It is definitions such
as this that lead people to think of humility as a
cringing, obsequious attitude that, to say the least,
is unappealing and unattractive. We cannot learn
how to develop humility except by looking up.

For reading & meditation – Psalm 121:1-8

APRIL 7

Knowing who you are

*I have set you an example that you
should do as I have done for you.*
John 13:15

*T*o be humble you first of all have to know *who*
you are and to whom you belong. And you don't
know *who* you are until you know *whose* you are.
Humility begins with a sense of being rooted in
God – if you like, a consciousness of greatness.
The small-minded and high-minded dare not be
humble; they have too much to lose. Humility as
demonstrated by Jesus is a choice. Our Lord, knowing his greatness and relationship to his Father,
made the choice to wash his disciples' feet. Being
in God made him great – and humble. He was
humble because he was great, and great because
he was humble.

For reading & meditation – John 13:1-17

APRIL 8

The garment of humility

All of you, clothe yourselves with humility ...
1 Peter 5:5

*O*ne of the most humble men I have ever met was also one of the most educated men I have ever encountered. When I asked him how he was able to avoid the arrogance that seems to be characteristic of so many who are highly educated he said: "The more I know about any subject the more I realise how much I do not know. That realisation helps me keep my place – at the feet of the Creator." A mind characterised by humility is a mind that has no arrogance, no self-consciousness, and exhibits a greater concern for others than for oneself. This is the way Christ's mind functioned.

For reading & meditation – 1 Peter 5:1-14

APRIL 9

Standing alone

*... put on the full armour of God, so that ...
you may be able to stand your ground ...*
Ephesians 6:13

*W*hat might be the third characteristic of a Christian mind? This – a perceptiveness that sees when to go along with the crowd and when to stand alone. We like to be together, we try to protect each other from common enemies such as fire, floods, natural disasters, and so on. But as Christians our final allegiance is not to others; it is to God. For this reason we must be prepared to break away from the herd if we see it going in the wrong direction. Those with a truly Christian mind have never hesitated to do this.

For reading & meditation – Ephesians 6:10-24

APRIL 10

~·//·~

Fear of others

*The king was distressed, but because of
his oaths and his dinner guests, he
ordered that her request be granted ...*
Matthew 14:9

*W*e are members of society, yet we must not be
dominated by it. Take the case of Herod outlined
in the passage before us today. He made a foolish
oath to give the daughter of Herodias almost anything she asked. When she asked for the head of
John the Baptist the account says: "because of his
oaths and his dinner guests, [Herod] ordered that
her request be granted." Note the phrase *and his
dinner guests*. Not the fear of God but the fear of
others determined his conduct and left him a
miserable murderer of the man he respected most.

For reading & meditation – Matthew 14:1-12

APRIL   11

Everybody does it

Everything they do is done for men to see ...
Matthew 23:5

*U*nless we are careful, the herd appeal can be so strong that we blindly follow it – to our peril. I talked to a young Christian couple a while ago who told me that though unmarried, they lived together. I waited for the appropriate moment to share with them my understanding of Scripture on this point, and when I did their reply was this: "But everybody does it these days – even Christians." I said: "It may suit you to believe everybody does it, but that is not true. Some may, but not everybody." "Everybody does it" is the last gurgle you will hear as men and women are submerged by the herd.

For reading & meditation – Matthew 23:1-23

APRIL 12

God's favour first

*Give to Caesar what is Caesar's,
and to God what is God's.*
Matthew 22:21

"*T*ell us," the Pharisees asked, "Is it right to pay taxes to Caesar or not?" If Jesus had said "No" he would have been in trouble with the authorities. If he had said "Yes" he would have been in trouble with the people. The answer he gave cut straight through the manoeuvring of his enemies and validated this statement: "You aren't swayed by men, because you pay no attention to who they are" (v. 16). He sought God's favour first and last, and as a result gained more favour than any other being who has set foot on this planet. He came and knelt at our feet; now we kneel at his.

For reading & meditation – Matthew 22:15-22

APRIL 13

Emancipated

Do not love the world or anything in the world.
1 John 2:15

*T*he Christian mind sees issues clearly and perceptively and says when necessary: this is not something the Lord wants me to do even though others are doing it. The supreme example of One who identified with the herd and yet was emancipated from it is, of course, Jesus. He identified with humanity so deeply that their sorrows became his sorrows, their sufferings his sufferings, which he took ultimately to the cross. He belonged to the human race but he belonged also to God. And with that supreme allegiance intact he went into the herd – emancipated. So must we.

For reading & meditation – 1 John 2:7-17

APRIL 14

A difficult test

Be strong and courageous, and do the work.
1 Chronicles 28:20

Some people get lost in the herd because they don't see any other way in which they can go. A test paper given to some young men who wanted to be accepted for the police force in London asked questions about problems that they might encounter. The last question on the test paper was: "How would you proceed to deal with the situation?" One applicant wrote: "I would slip out of my uniform and get lost in the crowd!" The mentality that wants to get lost in the crowd is not a Christian mentality. A true Christian refuses to escape into anonymity.

For reading & meditation – 1 Chronicles 28:11-21

APRIL 15

The bowed head

*Remind the people to be subject
to rulers and authorities ...*
Titus 3:1

*W*e look now at the fourth mark of a Christian
mind – its acceptance of the principle of authority. The Christian mind has to come to grips with
the fact that the principle of authority has been
built into the universe by God, and unless we
recognize this fact and understand it we will never
be able, as Paul put it in 1 Timothy 6:13-14, to
"keep our commission free from stain" (Moffatt).
As Christ's disciples we have been commissioned
to live out our lives according to the revelation
given to us in the Scriptures.

For reading & meditation – Titus 3:1-11

APRIL 16

Perfect freedom

*Now have come ... the power and the kingdom
of our God, and the authority of his Christ.*
Revelation 12:10

*I*n Berlin some years ago I gave a talk on the need
for Christians to bring themselves under the authority of Scripture and to submit to it in every
way. Afterwards several young people came up to
speak to me and commented politely: "We have
been set free from one totalitarianism; you seem
to be offering us another." I replied: "True, but
there is a profound difference. When you obey an
earthly totalitarian regime you find yourself in
bondage; when you obey the laws of the Bible and
the kingdom of God you find yourself in perfect
freedom."

For reading & meditation – Revelation 12:1-12

APRIL 17

A demand or an offer?

*... any of you who does not give up
everything he has cannot be my disciple.*
Luke 14:33

*A*s the stomach and poison are not made for each other, and when brought together produce disruption and death, so life and other-than-the-kingdom ways are not made for each other, and when brought together also produce disruption and death. What is the stomach made for? Is it not food? When food and stomach are brought together health and vitality develop. The kingdom of God is the food for which our nature craves, and when the kingdom and our nature are brought together then we experience life, health, and perfect fulfilment.

For reading & meditation – Luke 14:25-35

APRIL 18

What saith Scripture?

All Scripture is God-breathed and is
useful for teaching, rebuking, correcting
and training in righteousness ...
2 Timothy 3:16

*I*t is obvious to many that the spirit of the world –
the spirit of anti-authority – is creeping into the
modern-day Church. High-ranking spiritual leaders are calling into question the authority of the
Scriptures, and seem to be approaching God with
the attitude: "You ask too much of our reason. Let's
discuss the issues further and see if we can come
up with a compromise." I tell you with all the conviction of my being – this attitude is fatal to the
growth and development of the Christian Church.

For reading & meditation – 2 Timothy 3:10-17

I must be free

You have been set free from sin and
have become slaves to righteousness.
Romans 6:18

Many think – erroneously I have to say – that Christ's rule and freedom of thought are incompatible. "How can our will be said to be free," they question, "if we are told what to do before we even think of doing it?" Or: "If controls are placed on how we behave then we are not free." But the only way the mind can be free is to come under the authority of truth. The mind is not free, for example, when it is believing lies. On the contrary, it is in bondage to fantasy and falsehood. We are free, really free, only when our hearts and minds are submitted to the authority that guides the universe.

For reading & meditation – Romans 6:15-23

APRIL 20

The principle of authority

*... for there is no authority except
that which God has established.*
Romans 13:1

"*W*hat is important is not so much that you
get out from under that authority but that you learn
how to respond to it in a way that will develop
your character and help you to become the kind of
person God wants you to be. Anyone who can't
submit to authority will never be able to wield
authority." If they could see how God was using
the principle of authority as a kind of an emery-
wheel to polish their characters and prepare them
for responsibility in his kingdom, they would
begin to view the situation entirely differently.

For reading & meditation – Romans 13:1-14

Danger signs

I urge ... that requests ... be made for everyone – for kings and all those in authority ...
1 Timothy 2:1,2

A startling survey conducted recently among a group of churches in the United Kingdom showed that the majority of people polled thought those in non-Christian religions would get into heaven as long as they were sincere and lived a good life. But what does the Bible say? "Salvation is found in no-one else for there is no other name under heaven given to men by which we must be saved" (Acts 4:12). Christians must be on their guard, for there is clear evidence that our thinking is being influenced by the thinking of the world.

For reading & meditation – 1 Timothy 2:1-15

APRIL 22

A disciplined mind

*You ... were called to be free. But do not use your
freedom to indulge the sinful nature ...*
Galatians 5:13

"*D*ependence plus discipline," it has been said,
"makes for dependable disciples." This combina-
tion was brought home to me in a humorous way
some years ago when I heard a woman say that
after prayer she had been healed of arthritis in her
legs. Then she prayed again: "Lord, you have
healed me of arthritis, now what are you going to
do about my overweight?" The answer she received
was: "This kind goeth not out but by prayer and
fasting." Where only dependence could heal, that
was the answer. Where only discipline could heal,
that was the answer.

For reading & meditation – Galatians 5:1-18

Love that springs

The goal of this command is love,
which comes from a pure heart ...
1 Timothy 1:5

*A*gain I make the point – freedom comes through obedience to law. I have always liked the definition of freedom that goes like this: "Freedom is not the right to do what we want, but the power to do what we ought." Love can only "spring" – be spontaneous – when it comes from a pure heart, a good conscience, and a sincere faith. In other words, from a disciplined life. Any supposed freedom that leaves us with an impure heart, a bad conscience, and an insincere faith ends not in springing and singing, but in sighing and dying.

For reading & meditation – 1 Timothy 1:1-17

APRIL 24

A mind set on God

*Wait for the Lord; be strong and
take heart and wait for the Lord.*
Psalm 27:14

*T*here is a good deal of misunderstanding concerning prayer in the Christian Church. Some people think of it as the means by which we get God to do things for us. That is not the primary purpose of prayer. The primary purpose of prayer is to bring the whole of life into the presence of God for cleansing and decision-making. It is only the arrogant who think they can run their lives on the knowledge they gained during their years of education. If our minds are not set on God then we cannot have a Christian mindset. It is as simple as that.

For reading & meditation – Psalm 27:1-14

APRIL 25

The Lord is God

From heaven he made you hear
his voice to discipline you.
Deuteronomy 4:36

A great many good but ineffective people are
disciplined at the beginning of an undertaking but
fail to carry it through. Their lives are strewn with
the wreckage of good beginnings but poor end-
ings. Sometimes this is because they take up things
they shouldn't. Pray about everything that comes
along and ask God if he wants you to get involved
in it. Learn to say "No" to things which you are
not sure God wants you to get involved in. Save
yourself for the best. In Deuteronomy 12:13 we
read: "Be careful not to sacrifice your burnt offerings anywhere you please."

For reading & meditation – Deuteronomy 4:32-40

APRIL   26

It's nature

If we claim to be without sin, we deceive ourselves and the truth is not in us.
1 John 1:8

*T*here are no idols today, we are told. All have feet of clay. We are all the same. Some Christians say that this indicates a sense of sin. It does not. What it indicates is a sense of realism that urges us to take human nature as we find it. One magazine writer put it like this: "It's nature – and therefore hardly sin." This is the climate in which we find ourselves today. Let us be careful that we don't allow the modern passion for realism to brainwash us into taking human nature as we find it. If we say that we have no sin, says the Scripture, we deceive ourselves.

For reading & meditation – 1 John 1:1-10

APRIL 27

Look out for euphemisms

Who can say, "I have kept my heart
pure; I am clean and without sin?"
Proverbs 20:9

*W*atch out for euphemisms creeping into our language nowadays that describe sin by some other name. A lie is called a "fib". Adultery is called "love". Avoiding payment for something is described as "being smart". Sex before marriage is called a premarital sexual relationship. People of the world are glossing over the descriptions of sin which the Bible gives by using less offensive names. And that is one of the ways in which they grease the path to sin. It is so terribly easy to make a deadly thing innocuous by employing a light name.

For reading & meditation – Proverbs 20:1-12

APRIL 28

No excuse

*A man's own folly ruins his life, yet
his heart rages against the Lord.*
Proverbs 19:3

*T*he way of the world is to blame wrongdoing on difficult circumstances. We Christians must watch that we don't allow that same attitude to take root in our own minds. We must watch that we do not slip into the ways of the world and cultivate a mindset that justifies wrongdoing on the basis of circumstances. There is nothing so healthy, so disposing to spiritual growth than to drop all evasions and admit a fault. Circumstances are no excuse. Whatever else we may doubt let us not doubt that.

For reading & meditation – Proverbs 19:1-16

APRIL 29

A sin little talked about

Pride goes before destruction,
a haughty spirit before a fall.
Proverbs 16:18

*W*e must recognize that the secular mind, or as
some might describe it, the establishment, sees sin
and evil in quite different terms from the Christian mind. It was the establishment, we should
remember – the ruling class of the day – that
crucified our Lord. The true Christian mind will
go further than the secular mind in its definition of
evil, and will identify as one of the chief evils
something that is little talked about in the world –
pride. In the Christian moral system this is the sin
of all sins because it perverts the will and asserts
self as the centre of the universe.

For reading & meditation – Proverbs 16:1-20

A P R I L   30

MAY

He never lets go

The word of the Lord that came to Hosea ... during the reigns of Uzziah, Jotham, Ahaz and Hezekiah, kings of Judah, and ... of Jeroboam ... king of Israel.
Hosea 1:1

*T*here is in every human heart a deep longing to be loved. We are designed to be loved; built for it. And we long to be loved consistently – to be loved with a love that will never be taken away. The prophecy of Hosea introduces us to exactly that kind of love – a love that goes on loving despite all the frailties and weaknesses in the one who is loved. This undying love for which we all long can only be found in the heart of the Deity. God's love is a love that never lets go.

For reading & meditation – Hosea 1:1

MAY 1

God's marriage problem

When the Lord began to speak through Hosea, the Lord said to him, "Go, take to yourself an adulterous wife ..."
Hosea 1:2

*T*he vow Israel made with God was similar to a marriage vow. It was not long, however, before Israel had broken every one of the Ten Commandments and God appeared to leave her to her own devices. But divine love is a persistent love. "Help me, Hosea," the Almighty seems to be saying in this verse, "I have a marriage problem. Israel is my bride but she is unfaithful to me. Marry a prostitute. Love her as I love Israel. Perhaps she will see in your actions a picture of my own undying love."

For reading & meditation – Hosea 1:2

MAY 2

God's action man

So he married Gomer daughter of Diblaim,
and she conceived and bore him a son.
Hosea 1:3

*T*he Almighty had tried every way possible to save his marriage to the nation of Israel, but nothing had succeeded. There was no other way than for Hosea to put himself in a position where his abiding love for a promiscuous woman would become a visual aid to an equally promiscuous nation. When God's command came, Hosea appeared not to hesitate. Hosea knew the first rule of loving God is – obedience. Our relationship with God rises and falls at the point of obedience. When we stop obeying, God stops revealing.

For reading & meditation – Hosea 1:3

MAY 3

What's in a name?

*Then the Lord said to Hosea, "Call him Jezreel,
because I will soon punish the house of
Jehu for the massacre at Jezreel ..."*
Hosea 1:4

*D*espite the fact that Hosea's marriage to Gomer
was what someone has described as a "shotgun"
wedding, nevertheless they seemed to get off to a
good start. In due course a baby boy arrived and
as Hosea wondered what he should be called God
spoke to his heart and said, "Call him Jezreel",
which means "God scatters". The Almighty wanted
the message to come through his name that judge-
ment was about to fall on Israel for their unfaithfulness and idolatry.

For reading & meditation – Hosea 1:4-5

MAY 4

Near breaking point

... the Lord said to Hosea, "Call her Lo-Ruhamah,
for I will no longer show love to the house of
Israel, that I should at all forgive them."
Hosea 1:6

Not long after the arrival of Jezreel, a daughter is born to Hosea and Gomer, and God directs them to name her "Lo-Ruhamah", meaning "unloved". Casual readers of the Old Testament struggle with this and other similar pictures in which sometimes God's love appears to be as fickle as human love. However, it is important to realise that here the Lord is speaking in human language and is putting the case in the same way a husband might do after discovering his wife's unfaithfulness. This point must not be overlooked.

For reading & meditation – Hosea 1:6

M A Y   5

I have feelings too

After she had weaned Lo-Ruhamah,
Gomer had another son.
Hosea 1:8

*W*herever these youngsters went and whenever their names would be called, those with a functioning conscience would be reminded that the situation between God and his bride was serious. Israel really had no right to God's love. She had fallen for pagan gods. How could she claim that the Almighty was her Husband? When the people of God are tempted to turn from dependency on the Almighty and put their trust in other gods, we would, I believe, be less prone to failure if we remembered that the most awful thing about infidelity is not so much that it breaks God's laws, but that it breaks his heart.

For reading & meditation – Hosea 1:8-9

MAY 6

Judgment – not God's last word

Yet the Israelites will be like the sand on the sea-shore, which cannot be measured or counted.
Hosea 1:10

*H*osea receives a new directive from heaven. Israel "will be like the sand on the seashore, which cannot be measured or counted." Judgment is not God's last word – love is. The divine heart will seek to save the marriage despite all the hurt, anguish and pain. God acknowledged his feelings of frustration and anger but then he brought to mind his previous promise of commitment and proceeded to act – not on his feelings but on what he knew was right. That is the divine way. With God's help it must be ours too.

For reading & meditation – Hosea 1:10

MAY 7

The surprise of grace

In the place where it was said to them,
'You are not my people,' they will be
called 'sons of the living God.'
Hosea 1:10b

*T*hough the first chapter of Hosea begins with the delineation of the sins of God's bride, it ends with some of the most hope-filled words to be found anywhere in Scripture. It is what I can only describe as the surprise of grace. Those who were "not my people" will be called "the sons of the living God". Somehow, bent and broken Israel will be brought back into shape and both Israel and Judah will be reunited. God is adept at taking situations that are dark with defeat and turning them into triumphs.

For reading & meditation – Hosea 1:10-11

MAY 8

A change of names

*Say of your brothers, "My people",
and of your sisters, "My loved one".*
Hosea 2:1

*A*s you well know, it is the people you love who can hurt you the most. If a stranger rebuffs you it is quickly forgotten, but if a close friend clashes with you, the pain continues for days, weeks and, if there is no reconciliation, the pain continues in the soul, sometimes for years. The Almighty may be pained when his people go astray but he is never seen as wringing his hands in despair. Divine concern must never be interpreted as self-pity. How reassuring it is to know that God is not against us for our sin but for us against our sin. Or, to put it in a more familiar way – he hates sin, but loves the sinner.

For reading & meditation – Hosea 2:1

MAY 9

Tough love

Rebuke your mother, rebuke her, for she is not my wife, and I am not her husband. Let her remove the adulterous look from her face ...
Hosea 2:2

*T*he main thrust of this second chapter is God's complaint against Israel in terms of the analogy of marriage. Most commentators take the view that whilst God is unfolding the story of Israel's adultery the same kind of thing is happening to Hosea and Gomer, and thus Israel and Gomer are to be seen in parallel. God shows himself as someone to be reckoned with. He may love his people as they are, but he loves them too much to let them stay as they are and is ready when necessary to give them a taste of "tough love".

For reading & meditation – Hosea 2:2-4

Beguiled by Baal

She said, "I will go after my lovers, who give me my food and my water, my wool and my linen, my oil and my drink."
Hosea 2:5b

*T*he god Baal was known as the god of fertility and many of the Israelites were beguiled by his apparent prowess in producing the good things of life – food, wine, water, and so on. Can anything be worse than unfaithfulness and the breaking of one's vows? Yet it is being done daily, both by those who are married to earthly partners and those who are married to the Lord. If we can't be faithful to our vows then how can we be faithful to anything? Is our meditation today a window or a mirror?

For reading & meditation – Hosea 2:5-6

M A Y   1 1

A new weapon?

Therefore I will block her path with thornbushes ...
Hosea 2:6a

*C*learly trouble is brewing for both brides –
Gomer and Israel. They are about to lose everything that is important – money, treasures, festivi-
ties, food and home. They will, as we shall see,
lose even their freedom and end up in bondage.
God takes a hand in the situation and says he will
put around them "a hedge of thorns" – a divine
restraint that will make it much harder for them to
pursue the course they had planned. As a result of
this, their lovers will lose interest in them. "She
will chase after her lovers but not catch them; she
will look for them but not find them."

For reading & meditation – Hosea 2:6-7

MAY 12

No short cuts

... I will wall her in so that she cannot find her way.
Hosea 2:6b

A missionary decided to pray a "hedge of thorns" around his son. Recognising that he was harbouring a resentment against God for not stopping his son becoming involved in drugs, he confessed it as a sin and received the cleansing of Christ. He spent an hour a day in prayer, asking God to save his son. A week later his son came home looking somewhat confused, and said he had got involved with a drug ring but he had lost interest in them and they in him. Three clear steps: confession of sin, binding Satan's power and persistent prayer.

For reading & meditation – Hosea 2:6-7

MAY 13

An unhurried judge

*So now I will expose her lewdness before the eyes of
her lovers; no-one will take her out of my hands.*
Hosea 2:10

*T*he Canaanites were deeply interested in life; they
wanted it to be extended as long as possible and to
be constantly renewed. They wanted to encourage
new life in Mother Earth. If they produced new
life in the wombs of sacred prostitutes surely Baal
would get the message. Is it strange that Israel –
and reading between the lines Gomer also – are to
receive judgment? It would be stranger if they
didn't. God's judgments may not always be swift
but they are always sure.

For reading & meditation – Hosea 2:8-13

MAY 14

Thank God for trouble

*Therefore I am now going to allure her; I will lead
her into the desert and speak tenderly to her.*
Hosea 2:14

*I*s God too harsh with us when he allures us into
the desert? Not at all. The Divine Lover does it
because sometimes that is the only way he can get
our attention. Notice that when he gets us there he
speaks tenderly to us: "Can't you see that you are
not only hurting me but hurting yourself by the
way you have been living? Will you not stop and
consider that the way I plan for you to live is the
way that is best for you? My way is not alien to
your personality. You were made for happiness but
true happiness can only be found in me."

For reading & meditation – Hosea 2:14-17

MAY 15

Only one answer

*"In that day," declares the Lord, "you
will call me 'my husband'; you will no
longer call me 'my master'."*
Hosea 2:16

*G*od would allow Israel to be sold to foreigners
and become a slave but at the right time God would
step in, rescue his bride and reconcile her to himself. Then he would say, "You are my people" and
they would say, "You are my God." Why should
God go to such endless lengths to win back his
bride? There is only one answer – love. Not pity,
not the urge to show he cannot be beaten. Not even
the desire to overcome sin. It is love; sheer
unadulterated, inextinguishable love. A love that
simply will not let go.

For reading & meditation – Hosea 2:16-23

MAY   16

Out of this world

The Lord said to me, "Go, show your
love to your wife again ... Love her
as the Lord loves the Israelites ..."
Hosea 3:1

*I*n this short chapter, God commands the prophet
to take again his adulterous wife and pick up their
relationship where it had been left off. One commentator describes the love that was asked of
Hosea as "heroic". Another says, "It was the kind
of love that was out of this world." That was exactly what it was meant to picture – a love out of
this world. Hosea captures, as no other prophet
does, the tremendous power of divine love – a love
that goes on seeking to win the wandering heart
back to himself and refuses to give up.

For reading & meditation – Hosea 3:1

MAY 17

Lesson No. 1

*So I bought her for fifteen shekels of silver
and about a homer and a lethek of barley.*
Hosea 3:2

*W*hen Hosea set out to find Gomer and reinstate
her in the family home, he found her at the end of
her tether – in fact a slave's tether. After Hosea
pays the purchase price for his slave wife, the next
question is: how is he going to piece together their
broken relationship? To Gomer, love was something merely physical – being pawed by someone
who would pay the right price. Hosea knew
differently. I think Hosea's reason for sexual
abstinence was to attempt to teach her the
difference between love and lust – love can always
wait to give, lust can never wait to get.

For reading & meditation – Hosea 3:2-3

In good hands

*For the Israelites will live for many days
without king or prince, without sacrifice
or sacred stones, without ephod or idol.*
Hosea 3:4

*L*ike Gomer, Israel was hooked on the physical
side of life, and thought of love only in terms of
sensual feelings. Israel and Gomer were two of a
kind – they wanted love without having to give
love. They focused on getting rather than giving.
But there is to come a time of reckoning. Both
brides have to find out what love and marriage is
all about. Once again, however, we note that God's
last word is not judgment. When God made his
marriage vow to Israel at the foot of Sinai, he was
not pretending. He promised her paradise and one
day paradise is what she is going to get.

For reading & meditation – Hosea 3:4-5

M A Y   19

Breach of promise

*... the Lord has a charge to bring
against you who live in the land ...*
Hosea 4:1b

*F*aithfulness, love and knowledge – form the basis of any developing relationship. God can only
be known as a relationship with him is cultivated
and developed. And what he longs for above all –
is not simply the obedient acts of his people but a
close relationship with them. Sin is never seen in
its true light until it is seen not simply as violating
certain rules and regulations but as damaging a
relationship. And more is needed to rebuild a broken relationship than quick apologies and hasty
resolutions.

For reading & meditation – Hosea 4:1-3

A long, hot summer

*... the beasts of the field and the birds of
the air and the fish of the sea are dying.*
Hosea 4:3b

"*D*rought" was a terrifying word to the
Israelites. It conjured up in their minds all kinds
of problems – deprivation, destitution, poverty, and
many other things, including death. God cannot
stand back and allow his people to get away with
some of the vilest sins imaginable without
making it clear to them that if they continue to
remain unrepentant then they must suffer the
consequences. What in effect the Almighty was
saying was this: "Be warned – it's going to be a
long, hot summer." How sad that the people of
God have to be chastened into submission instead
of continually resting there.

For reading & meditation – Hosea 4:2-3

M A Y   21

Crooks in priest's clothing

... my people are destroyed from lack of knowledge.
Hosea 4:6a

*T*here was one group of people in Israel who needed to be singled out for condemnation – the priests. They perhaps more than any other group were responsible for the spiritual bankruptcy of the nation. They encouraged the people to disregard the Ten Commandments, and to flirt with pagan gods. They were nothing more than spiritual chameleons – matching their colour to the context. God tells both the people and the priests, "Enough is enough. I will punish both of them for their ways and repay them for their deeds." Be sure of this – every act of rebellion carries the Divine Government health warning: "Sin now, pay later."

For reading & meditation – Hosea 4:4-9

MAY 22

The only way back

They will eat but not have enough ...
Hosea 4:10a

*J*ust how will God go about the task of punishing and disciplining both the priests and the people? Hosea quotes an old Israelite proverb: "A people without understanding will come to ruin!" (v. 14b). Probably a more literal translation of the Hebrew words would sound like this: "A people who won't think, won't survive." How can such a people regain their spiritual understanding? There is only one way – repentance. To repent means to rethink one's position, to realise one's foolishness and return to God with a sorrowful heart and a contrite spirit. Once we move away from God this is the only way back.

For reading & meditation – Hosea 4:10-14

MAY 23

The power of irony

Ephraim is joined to idols; leave him alone!
Hosea 4:17

*H*osea's indictment of Israel now takes an ironical twist. Instead of addressing Israel, he turns his attention to neighbouring Judah and exhorts them not to visit Israel or patronise their favourite shrines. To understand what Hosea is saying here, imagine a multifaith service in, say, Westminster Abbey where Jehovah, Buddha and Mohammed are worshipped simultaneously. Of such a service Hosea would say: "Go to Westminster Abbey and blaspheme." How can the Lord pasture such stubborn, obstinate sheep? The prodigal son (to change the metaphor) must be left for a while to wallow in the pig-swill. Nothing else will make him come to himself.

For reading & meditation – Hosea 4:15-19

MAY   24

Faith torn and bleeding

Hear this, you priests! Pay attention, you Israelites!
Listen, O royal house! ... You have been a snare at
Mizpah, a net spread out on Tabor.
Hosea 5:1

I wonder what Hosea would say, were he alive today and saw the spiritual apostasy in some of our churches and theological training institutions. Many a young minister entering a seminary nowadays goes in with faith and confidence in the Gospel and comes out with uncertainty and doubt. There are equivalents to Mizpah and Tabor in our contemporary Christian society. If I had Hosea's courage I might even name them. God would not leave Israel without a day of reckoning, and a day of reckoning will come for these modern counterparts as well.

For reading & meditation – Hosea 5:1-2

M A Y   25

Taking God seriously

*Their deeds do not permit them to return to their
God. A spirit of prostitution is in their heart;
they do not acknowledge the Lord.*
Hosea 5:4

*W*hen there is no knowledge of God, then religion becomes a matter of ceremony and ritual. We have a picture of people going through all the due process of religion and yet God is not listening to them. "When they go with their flocks and herds to seek the Lord," says Hosea, "they will not find him." How tragic. Nothing can be more terrible than to talk or plead with the Lord and for him not to answer. And why? Because our Lord does not trifle with those who do not take him seriously.

For reading & meditation – Hosea 5:3-6

God's silent judgments

I am like a moth to Ephraim,
like rot to the people of Judah.
Hosea 5:12

*C*onsider the word-pictures Hosea conjures up as he describes the impending judgment: "I will pour out my wrath on them like a flood of water ... I am like a moth to Ephraim." Language is being used here to show that God not only sends judgment with a great show of power (like a flood of water) but silently also – "like a moth". We must not think because there are no signs of outward judgment that God's sentences are not being carried out. It is an illusion. You can be sure that God's judgments are silently at work on the inside. It is inevitable, God being Who he is.

For reading & meditation – Hosea 5:7-12

MAY 27

~·*·~

Productive misery

... in their misery they will earnestly seek me.
Hosea 5:15b

*H*ow sad and hurt God must feel when his people resort to every other means to save themselves rather than humbly repent and turn to him. The lengths to which the people of God will go rather than humble themselves before the Lord is astonishing. It is a sad comment on our human condition that God has to make us miserable before we seek his face. This is what C.S. Lewis describes as a "severe mercy" – God allowing difficult circumstances to come upon us in order to draw us more closely to himself.

For reading & meditation – Hosea 5:13-15

MAY 28

Facile praying

Come, let us return to the Lord. He has torn
us to pieces but he will heal us; he has injured
us but he will bind up our wounds.
Hosea 6:1

*A*t first glance, these words might suggest that
Hosea is leading the people in a prayer of repentance but most commentators view it as Israel's
own words used in a facile and presumptuous way.
The people of God, covenant people remember,
seemed to have no idea of what faithful love was
all about. They made light of their own spiritual
state and of the agony that God felt over their un-
requited love. It is a broken marriage that God is
concerned about here, not just a little tiff between
friends.

For reading & meditation – Hosea 6:1-3

M A Y   29

God remembers

Their sins engulf them; they are always before me.
Hosea 7:2b

*T*he spiritual and the social are much more intertwined than many realise. I wish some of our befuddled politicians would recognise this. Many of them say, "What a man or woman does privately bears no relation to their work." Doesn't it? If a man cheats on his wife (or vice versa) then can he be trusted not to cheat his employer? People think that personal guilt and national guilt fade away with time. They don't. Sin, whether it is in the Church or in a nation, stares God in the face. And it stays there, insulting him, unless there is real repentance.

For reading & meditation – Hosea 6:4-7:2

M A Y   30

Righteous anger

Their hearts are like an oven; they approach him with intrigue. Their passion smoulders all night; in the morning it blazes like a flaming fire.
Hosea 7:6

*I*t is important to realise that Hosea, being a true prophet, was concerned not only with exposure but also with restoration. A preacher or teacher who delights in announcing judgment but has no heart for restoration is not following the biblical pattern. What we are seeing in God's pronouncements of judgment on Israel is not spite or spleen, but righteous anger. Righteous anger directed toward the good of others, not just spite or spleen at what is happening to oneself. God's judgments on his people are not retributive, but remedial.

For reading & meditation – Hosea 7:3-7

MAY   31

JUNE

Able to keep

... where does my help come from?
My help comes from the Lord ...
Psalm 121:1-2

*W*hat do we do when, on the walk of faith, we meet with some major difficulty or trip over some obstruction? Often when in trouble we scan the horizon hoping that someone will appear and come to our aid. However, the psalmist is making the point that we should not look to the hills for help but to the God of the hills. The panacea we need when troubles come is not to be found in nature. It can be a wonderful supplement but never a substitute. When troubles come we must look much higher than the hills. *Our help comes from the Lord.*

For reading & meditation – Psalm 121:1-8

JUNE 1

Me! Me! Me!

Woe to them, because they have strayed from me! ... they have rebelled against me! ... they speak lies against me.
Hosea 7:13

*H*ear once again the pain in God's heart as he cries: "they have strayed from me! ... they have rebelled against me! ... they speak lies against me ... they do not cry out to me." Israel was God's strongbow, designed to aim the arrows of truth into the midst of the pagan nations. But now the bow was badly bent. God intended that Israel should convert the pagans, but instead the pagans had converted Israel. How does God deal with his people when they are bent on going against him? They must be judged. And remember it is not hatred that guides him, but love.

For reading & meditation – Hosea 7:13-16

JUNE 2

Our choices v. his choices

*This calf – a craftsman has made it; it is not God. It
will be broken in pieces, that calf of Samaria.*
Hosea 8:6b

*H*ow did Israel react to the warnings given them
by God? Typically they said, "O God, we acknowledge you!" (v.2). The bride claimed to acknowledge her husband but God knew better. First, the
people have rejected "good". Kevin Logan points
out that "good" is the long way of spelling "God".
"To reject good," he says, "is to reject God."
Second, they chose their own kings (v.4). Third,
they created their own gods (vv. 4-6). The people
collected together their silver and gold and went
into the god-manufacturing business. First off the
production line was a golden calf. Memories of
Sinai here?

For reading & meditation – Hosea 8:1-6

JUNE 3

The world in the Church

They sow the wind and reap the whirlwind. The stalk has no head; it will produce no flour. Were it to yield grain, foreigners would swallow it up.
Hosea 8:7

*W*hen we sow the wind, we bring upon us disastrous results. What a powerful lesson this provides for the contemporary Christian Church. We are not to ignore the world nor cut ourselves off from society, but we are to be careful in our contact with them. We need to approach the world with motives that are pure and not allow ourselves to become intrigued or entangled in its webs of duplicity and deceit. God put the Church in the world but we must watch that the devil doesn't put the world in the Church.

For reading & meditation – Hosea 8:7-10

JUNE 4

God hates pretence

Though Ephraim built many altars for sin offerings, these have become altars for sinning.
Hosea 8:11

*W*e come now to an indictment that is perhaps one of the most damning of all – the altars that had been built in order to take away sin had now become altars at which sin was being committed. How sad that the very thing designed to take away sin was now being used to increase sin. Nothing can be more offensive to God than to pretend on the outside to be engaged in worshipping him but inside to be detached and indifferent. All the Old Testament prophets combine to show us that God hates pretence, especially when it appears at his altars.

For reading & meditation – Hosea 8:11-14

JUNE 5

The root of sin

Israel has forgotten his Maker and built palaces; Judah has fortified many towns ...
Hosea 8:14

*H*ad not God knocked down the walls of Jericho for the people when they first entered the land? Someone has said that spiritual maturity can be measured by where we put our trust. Is it in God or in things? In the Saviour or in silver? In God or in gold? There is nothing wrong, of course, in wealth or in having a healthy bank account. But that is not where we put our trust. Our trust must be in the Lord. He can soon blow on wealth and it will end up, as Haggai said, like putting coins in a bag full of holes (Haggai 1:6).

For reading & meditation – Hosea 8:14

JUNE 6

Get ready to be shocked

Do not rejoice, O Israel; do not be
jubilant like the other nations. For you
have been unfaithful to your God ...
Hosea 9:1

*T*he apostle James uses a startling expression
when he says that any Christian who flirts with
the world is an "adulterer" (James 4:4). An adulterer? Surely not. A fool perhaps. Or shallow. But
an *adulterer*? Yes, an adulterer – someone who
gives themself in a close relationship with someone other than their spouse. But James goes even
further. "Friendship with the world," he says, "is
hatred towards God." Adulterer! Hatred towards
God! These are shocking words. But then that is
what worldly minded believers need. They need
to be shocked.

For reading & meditation – Hosea 9:1-6

JUNE 7

God's watchman

... the prophet is considered a fool ...
Hosea 9:7b

*I*t is said of certain parts of history that when a messenger brought bad news to a king he was sometimes beheaded for his pains. Hosea's announcement to Israel that the party was over, and judgment was about to fall was greeted not with active violence but with passive contempt. They simply called him a fool, a maniac. The people may have thought of Hosea as a fool, but God has another name for him – "a watchman". A watchman, according to Ezekiel 33:1-9, was someone who stood on the walls of a city and heralded the approach of an enemy. If the announcement of the watchman was ignored, the city would risk being overrun by the enemy.

For reading & meditation – Hosea 9:7-9

JUNE 8

Tough stuff

*... they consecrated themselves to that shameful idol
and became as vile as the thing they loved.*
Hosea 9:10b

*O*ne of the first turning points in Israel's relationship with God came at Shittim when the
Israelite men indulged in immorality with the
Moabite women and worshipped their gods
(Numbers 25). Hosea tells us that when they did
this they became "as vile as the thing they loved".
The Israelites had looked sin full in the face and
they had become as vile as the thing they had indulged in. Don't feel sympathetic toward Israel.
She is going to get what she deserved. This is tough
stuff, but God is going to see the matter through
to the bitter end. Israel must take God's cure or
take the consequences.

For reading & meditation – Hosea 9:10-14

JUNE   9

The long look

*Because of all their wickedness
in Gilgal, I hated them there.*
Hosea 9:15a

*O*ne of the most hallowed spots in Israel was Gilgal. It was the place where Joshua set up twelve stones to celebrate the successful crossing of the Jordan and thus became Israel's first place of worship in the Promised Land. What exactly happened at Gilgal that caused God to say, "I hated them there" is something about which we cannot be certain. God hates in a different way from us, with no pique and no animosity. He hates the sin but loves the sinner. And the expression of his hatred is not to make himself feel better but for his people's good.

For reading & meditation – Hosea 9:15-17

JUNE 10

The evil of syncretism

Israel was a spreading vine; ... As
his fruit increased, he built more altars; ...
Hosea 10:1

*M*any years ago, I did a study of all the warnings contained in both Old and New Testaments and I was staggered at the result. God gives his people clear information on what will happen if they disobey, so that no one caught up in his disciplines can say, "I didn't realise the consequences." But look with me now at the opening verse in which God speaks of Israel as a spreading (or luxuriant) vine. The more they prospered physically the more they declined spiritually. The same thing is being done nowadays by some churches who advocate the celebration of different religions.

For reading & meditation – Hosea 10:1

JUNE 11

Weeping over an idol

Its people will mourn over it ...
Hosea 10:5b

*M*orality that is not rooted in God is a morality that is inadequate to hold people together. "Lawsuits spring up like poisonous weeds in a ploughed field" (v. 4). Couldn't these same words be said of contemporary society in which biblical values are choked and humanistic values abound as poisonous weeds? Note this also: in Samuel's day, Israel's tears had been for the captured ark of the covenant, but now the people will shed tears over a captured idol – the calf idol erected at Beth Aven (v. 5). Can anything be more sad than seeing the glory of God exchanged for an idol?

For reading & meditation – Hosea 10:2-6

JUNE 12

Powerful word - pictures

Then they will say to the mountains,
"Cover us!" and to the hills, "Fall on us!"
Hosea 10:8b

*H*osea's use of metaphors and similes is something we have had occasion to comment on a number of times and, once again, he puts together three powerful word-pictures that unfold in graphic terms the problems that lay ahead for rebellious Israel. Hosea's word-picture is that of people crying for the mountains and hills to cover them (v. 8). Here we see shades of the horror that struck Jerusalem a generation after our Lord had been crucified. Christ used these very words, you remember, as he made his way to Calvary: "they will say to the mountains, 'Fall on us!' and to the hills 'Cover us!'" (Luke 23:30).

For reading & meditation – Hosea 10:7-10

JUNE 13

What time is it?

Sow for yourselves righteousness, ...
and break up your unploughed ground;
for it is time to seek the Lord ...
Hosea 10:12

*G*od is now about to put a different yoke upon Israel's neck – the yoke of bondage and slavery (v. 11b). A yoke is there to enable an animal to go in the right direction, and Israel's new yoke would have a similar purpose in the mind of God. The phrases: "Sow for yourselves righteousness ... break up your unploughed ground" have been used on countless occasions down the years by preachers calling the Church back to repentance; and particularly the phrase, "it is time to seek the Lord" (v. 12). In other words, "there is very little time left."

For reading & meditation – Hosea 10:11-15

JUNE 14

Divine nostalgia

When Israel was a child, I loved him,
and out of Egypt I called my son.
Hosea 11:1

The chapter which now engages our attention has been described by one commentator as: "one of the boldest in the Old Testament". His reason for saying this is because "it exposes us to the mind and heart of God in human terms." God now describes himself as a parent grieving over his rebellious child. Some Christians have difficulty with the figure of God as a Father because their own experience of an earthly father has been negative, and thus they form a negative image of fatherhood and tend to project that selfsame image on to God.

For reading & meditation – Hosea 11:1-3

JUNE 15

An agonised cry

How can I give you up, Ephraim?
Hosea 11:8a

*H*ow could anyone turn away from such a love as this? That is what Israel did, however, but God is committed to his people and, no matter what, he will not give them up. The very thought of forsaking his people and abandoning them to their plight arouses deep feelings in the heart of the Almighty. His big heart is caught up in a tremendous tug-of-war. Justice pulls in one direction and mercy in the other. Does God have emotion? Let the question never come up again. The Almighty anguishes over his people's infidelities, grieves over their wandering affections, and cries out in pain when his marriage shows signs of breaking down.

For reading & meditation – Hosea 11:4-8

Words of promise

"I will settle them in their homes," declares the Lord.
Hosea 11:11b

*W*e saw yesterday how the great heart of God was caught up in a tremendous tug-of-war. Now we see how God has decided: "I will not carry out my fierce anger, nor will I turn and devastate Ephraim" (v. 9). This must not be taken to mean that God had changed his mind about disciplining the people; what it meant was that he would not destroy them or cast them away. The people of God would find themselves in the furnace of affliction but they would survive and have a future. Troubles still assail Israel, and always will, until the day comes in the future when through a radical and national repentance she will enter into a deep, intimate relationship with God once again.

For reading & meditation – Hosea 11:9-11

JUNE   17

Right and wrong – universal

Ephraim feeds on the wind; he pursues the east
wind all day and multiplies lies and violence ...
Hosea 12:1

*O*nce again using word-pictures to describe Ephraim's double-talk and double-dealing – "Ephraim feeds on the wind" – Hosea warns that such deceit has not gone unnoticed by God. Double-talk, double-dealing and lies always end in disaster, wherever they are practised. The laws that govern right and wrong are of universal application. Malcolm Muggeridge put it best when he said, "Truth and honesty have their source in the bosom of God and their voices when heard bring harmony to the world."

For reading & meditation – Hosea 11:12-12:1

JUNE 18

A strange wrestling match

The Lord has a charge to bring against Judah; he will punish Jacob according to his ways ...
Hosea 12:2

*A*fter years of trickery, God finally caught up with the supplanter and arranged an extraordinary wrestling match between Jacob and one of his angels. Jacob came off worse and ended up with a limp which was with him for the rest of his life. But as a result of the contest he became a new man. The point of the story is: "... you must return to your God; maintain love and justice, and wait for your God always." Israel's nature could not be changed apart from an encounter with God.

For reading & meditation – Hosea 12:2-6

Why are we redeemed?

*I am the Lord your God, who brought you out of
Egypt; I will make you live in tents again ...*
Hosea 12:9

*W*hat's wrong with finger tipping the scales now
and again? Or purloining a few odds and ends from
work that nobody will miss? Or cheating on a tax
return? This is God's paraphrased answer: "Is this
what I redeemed you for, brought you out of Egypt
for – that you be no better than the Canaanite? If
that's the case then you had better go back to
living in tents!" How sad it is when Christians who
have been brought out of the world live no better
than the people of the world. Is this what we have
been redeemed for?

For reading & meditation – Hosea 12:7-9

JUNE 20

Moses – prophet or leader?

The Lord used a prophet to bring Israel up from Egypt, by a prophet he cared for him.
Hosea 12:13

*S*ome in Israel may have thought of Moses as a great leader but the Almighty makes clear here that his main ministry was not to stand before Pharaoh but to stand before God. He was a prophet first and a leader second. Thus the spiritual nature of the exodus (not merely a liberation movement) is underlined. God's point is therefore clear – at least clear now to us – it is no good having prophecy and not heeding it. When our appetite for truth fails because of lack of exercise and obedience then we are in the most desperate of conditions spiritually.

For reading & meditation – Hosea 12:10-14

JUNE 21

Kissing calves

*It is said of these people, "They offer
human sacrifice and kiss the calf-idols."*
Hosea 13:2b

*T*he Israelites had forgotten one important truth;
it is God who makes man, not man who makes
God. Earlier you will remember (Hosea 6:4) God
likened the love of Ephraim and Judah to the morning mist – transient and temporary; now they are
seen also as "like chaff swirling from a threshing-
floor, like smoke escaping through a window" (v.
3). There is not much hope for people who have
no morals or no character. They may appear to be
prosperous for a while but their future is doomed.

For reading & meditation – Hosea 13:1-3

JUNE 22

Petty jealousy?

But I am the Lord your God, who brought
you out of Egypt. You shall acknowledge
no God but me, no Saviour except me.
Hosea 13:4

*O*ne liberally minded theologian describes God's threats here as "petty jealousy". Well, it is jealousy all right, but no "petty" jealousy. Divine jealousy must not be confused with human jealousy. Human jealousy is usually full of self-interest – this should not be happening to me. Divine jealousy is characterised by other-interest – this should not be happening to you. In God, jealousy is a fiery concern that others will attempt to give his people what he knows only he can give.

For reading & meditation – Hosea 13:4-8

JUNE 23

"Stored up" sin

The guilt of Ephraim is stored up,
his sins are kept on record.
Hosea 13:12

*Y*ou are familiar, no doubt, with the background of Israel's original demand for a king. Let's spend a few moments reflecting on it. The account is given in 1 Samuel 8. Israel began to tire of being led by an invisible God and wanted to have a visible leader like the other nations – a king. This was not God's wish but he allowed them to have a king nevertheless, and was prepared to bless this arrangement if they handled it properly. However, the people tended to worship the kings more than they did God and some of the kings that were appointed were so corrupt that they hindered rather than helped the people.

For reading & meditation – Hosea 13:9-13

JUNE 24

How can God do this?

I will have no compassion ...
Hosea 13:14c

*T*he springs will fail, the wells will dry up, Israel's storehouses will be plundered, people will perish by the sword and little children will be dashed to the ground. A God who so clearly is love, must have a good reason to allow such things to happen, and I should interpret the strange and mysterious actions of God by what I know about him through the Cross: I know God is love and, though I find it difficult to reconcile some of his judgments with the concept of his love, I believe that ultimately everything God does will be fully and perfectly justified. Therefore I take my stand with that of another who said, "Will not the Judge of all the earth do right?" (Gen. 18:25).

For reading & meditation – Hosea 13:14-16

J U N E   2 5

Repentance – the first step

> *Return, O Israel, to the Lord your God.*
> *Your sins have been your downfall!*
> Hosea 14:1

*I*srael can still escape death and live. She must return to the Lord. These opening verses of chapter 14 provide us with the best analysis of what is involved in spiritual repentance to be found anywhere in the Word of God. Follow it carefully with me. The next time you need to repent, you will be glad to have pondered the necessary elements of repentance. "Return, O Israel, to the Lord your God" (v. 1). The first thing we should know about repentance is that it involves returning to God.

For reading & meditation – Hosea 14:1

Words are important

Take words with you and return to the Lord. Say to him: "Forgive all our sins and receive us graciously, that we may offer the fruit of our lips."
Hosea 14:2

*W*e must be courageous enough to explore the depths of our sin, and clearly identify what needs to be confessed. The story of the Prodigal Son, recorded for us in Luke's Gospel, includes this. The son knew exactly what he was going to say to the father, and carefully rehearsed it before he made the long trek home. The more clear and thorough our awareness of our sin, the more complete and full our repentance. It is much, much more than a general commitment to change. Repentance becomes effective only when the general becomes the particular.

For reading & meditation – Hosea 14:2

JUNE 27

To live we must die

Assyria cannot save us ...
Hosea 14:3a

*W*e are very familiar now with Israel's spiritual condition. They were on the point of national catastrophe. But instead of turning to God for help they were more inclined to turn to Assyria. We do something similar when we resort to all kinds of defences to protect ourselves from the exposure that repentance inevitably demands. Our dependency is to be in God, and when it is put in anything other or less than him, then that thing becomes an idol. If all this sounds like the road to death – it is. But remember, according to Jesus, only he who is willing to die can live.

For reading & meditation – Hosea 14:3

J U N E   28

A happy ending

I will heal their waywardness and love them freely,
for my anger has turned away from them.
Hosea 14:4

Can there be a happy ending for Israel? Yes, there can. Following repentance, her life will not just be a bed of roses but of blossoming flowers! Israel had discarded God a long time ago and thus is as dry and arid as a desert, but one day God will come raining down on the Israelites so that the nation will become "like a cedar of Lebanon" (v. 5b). But there's more. "Israel's splendour will be like an olive tree, his fragrance like a cedar of Lebanon". She will also be as fruitful in her love as the fruitful vineyards are with grapes.

For reading & meditation – Hosea 14:4-7

JUNE 29

A postscript

Who is wise? He will realise these things. Who is discerning? He will understand them.
Hosea 14:9a

*H*osea's work is nearly done. He has put the case on God's behalf. But now comes a postscript. If were to paraphrase Hosea's postscript it would sound something like this: "If you have any sense at all, you will get the message. If you have any semblance of wisdom, you will take the point. And what is the point? This: those who walk with God walk safely; those who won't, have to stumble tragically on their own." If you take all that Hosea has said and apply it to your own relationship with Christ, then it will be pleasure and not pain that will fill your Saviour's heart.

For reading & meditation – Hosea 14:8-9

JUNE   30

JULY

What is a Christian?

I give them eternal life, and they shall never perish ...
John 10:28

A Christian is someone who has eternal life. This is the primary reason why God sent his Son into the world: "that he might give eternal life to all those you have given him." In John 17:3 our Lord explains just what eternal life is: "this is eternal life: that they may know you, the only true God, and Jesus Christ, whom you have sent." Eternal life, then, consists in *knowing* God. God can only be truly known when we approach him through his Son. Life, real life that is, cannot be found in any way except through Jesus Christ. It's so simple yet so wondrously sublime.

For reading & meditation – John 10:22-42

JULY 1

Heaven – "pie in the sky"?

*For Christ did not enter a man-made
sanctuary ... he entered heaven itself ...*
Hebrews 9:24

*D*uring the past few decades there has been such an emphasis on the "social gospel" that many of us are afraid to talk of heaven in case our belief is thought to be "pie in the sky". Well, let it be said right away that the "social gospel" is not the whole gospel. We must not neglect our responsibilities to the community, the nation and the world, and we must do everything we can to ease the plight of those who are deprived. However, we must never lose sight of the fact that the only "new Jerusalem" we shall see is not man-made but is eternal and in heaven.

For reading & meditation – Hebrews 9:11-28

JULY 2

Relaxed yet restless

*... the faith and love that spring from the
hope that is stored up for you in heaven ...*
Colossians 1:5

I contend that you will work the better for God
here on earth when, by faith, you have the perfect
end in view. So don't run away with the idea that
as I guide you through some devotional thinking
on the subject of heaven over the next few weeks
your impact for God here on earth will be les-
sened. Some in the past have become so preoccupied with heaven that they were then no earthly
good, but that need not happen to you. In fact, when
you hold the vision of heaven ever before you it
will spur you on in your work for God here below.

For reading & meditation – Colossians 1:1-14

The air of an exile

... the man who hates his life in this
world will keep it for eternal life.
John 12:25

I had the privilege once of knowing a man whom I consider the most Christlike person I have ever met. He was a coal miner, and what was astonishing was to see how non-Christians related to him. No one would curse or swear in his presence, and if perchance they forgot themselves and let slip a bad word they would instantly apologize. When he died almost everyone from the coal pit where he had worked attended his funeral. One of Wales's most famous preachers gave the funeral address. "Our brother," he said, "had about him the air of an exile."

For reading & meditation – John 12:20-36

JULY 4

Pilgrim on an inward Odyssey

... an inheritance that can never perish, spoil or fade – kept in heaven for you ...
1 Peter 1:4

*P*eter reminds his readers of the hope given to every believer of an inheritance that can never perish – *kept in heaven*: the more godly a person is the more aware he or she seems to be of heaven. Contrast this with the statement made by a well-known British author which I read in a magazine recently: "I have no interest in what lies beyond this life. Earth satisfies me." How sad. I certainly have not found all I want in this life. I have had a taste of heaven down here on earth, but it is only a taste. The full banquet comes later.

For reading & meditation – 1 Peter 1:1-9

JULY 5

God who is our home

He has also set eternity in the hearts of men ...
Ecclesiastes 3:11

*T*he text before us today suggests that when God designed us he put within us longings for immortality – a yearning for eternity. What has fascinated me over the years is to see how this simple but powerful fact makes itself known in people's lives. We were made by God for God, and there is a restlessness in us that will never go away until we find our home in God. All feel it but not all understand it. A man with whom I chatted recently when I was in Malaysia – a good and godly man – said to me: "Why is it that I never feel at home in this world?" I answered: "You were never meant to." Never.

For reading & meditation – Ecclesiastes 3:1-14

JULY 6

The ultimate disaster

*... Christ Jesus ... has destroyed death
and has brought life and immortality to
light through the gospel.*
2 Timothy 1:10

*T*he Christian message makes this longing for immortality, this hunger of the soul for home, clear
to us. And that is why this nostalgia for home is
understood aright only by those who have had their
hearts illuminated by the gospel. Most men and
women in the world don't quite know what is
wrong with them. They are aware there are times
when they want to be alone, when they look to the
calendar or the stars or death to speak to them.
They know they long for something. But what?
How grateful we should be that what we long for
has been made clear to us through the gospel.

For reading & meditation – 2 Timothy 1:1-12

JULY 7

The one common malady

Jesus stood and said in a loud voice, "If anyone is thirsty, let him come to me and drink."
John 7:37

*O*n one occasion I heard a Christian psychiatrist say: "Homesickness is the one common malady of mankind out of which all other problems emerge." What did he mean? I think he meant this: because God has built into us longings for himself there is something in all of us which the world cannot satisfy. Money will not satisfy it. Fame will not satisfy it. Pleasure will not satisfy it. Not even a father, mother, spouse or dearest friend can satisfy it. *What we long for in our souls simply cannot be provided by any earthly relationship.*

For reading & meditation – John 7:25-43

JULY 8

Inconsolable longings

Why spend money on what is not bread,
and your labour on what does not satisfy?
Isaiah 55:2

*I*f it is true that a longing for heaven has been built into the human heart, how does the great mass of humanity go about dealing with it? One way is to pretend this mysterious aspect of our existence does not exist. It is a strange fact of life that this aspect of human nature – the soul's deep sense of homelessness – is not studied more intently. I wonder why. Perhaps it's because it fits none of the usual categories of thought. It can't be labelled, sorted, explained or matched so men and women make a detour to avoid it and treat it as if it wasn't there. But the detour is really a denial.

For reading & meditation – Isaiah 55:1-13

Sit quietly before mystery

Be still, and know that I am God ...
Psalm 46:10

*H*uman beings have a tendency whenever they are unable to find an explanation for some matter to fit it into a category for which they do have an explanation. This passion to explain matters is our way of bringing them under our control. We feel less helpless and vulnerable when we are able to manage things than when we have to sit quietly before mystery. But the affairs of the soul cannot always be managed; they are best handled by sitting quietly before God in private prayer.

For reading & meditation – Psalm 46:1-11

JULY 10

None so blind ...

*... the sinful mind is hostile to God. It does
not submit to God's law, nor can it do so.*
Romans 8:7

*I*f you have ever read C.S. Lewis's *The Silver
Chair* you will be familiar with the section where
the beautiful Queen of the Underworld tries to convince the children from the Overworld that her
dismal kingdom is the only reality and their world
is but an imagined dream. "There is no sun," she
says. "You have seen my lamps and imagined that
there was a sun." Perhaps in the light of the text I
have chosen for today we should not blame unbelievers too much for their blindness. But there
again, as the saying goes: "There are none so blind
as those who do not wish to see."

For reading & meditation – Romans 8:1-17

JULY 11

Utopianism

*The heart is deceitful above all things and
beyond cure. Who can understand it?*
Jeremiah 17:9

*I*n the 1920s and 30s politicians fervently believed
they could bring about a state of perfection. "With
more advanced education," they said, "with increased knowledge, better understanding of social
forces, we are coming to the point where we should
be able to provide healthy, happy and useful lives
for all. The day is not far off when no need will
have to go unsatisfied and no child go unloved."
Then came World War II, after which we learned
that in one of the best educated societies of the
day millions of Jews had been gassed. There has
not been much talk of Utopia since.

For reading & meditation – Jeremiah 17:1-10

JULY 12

Just a stopover

*Remember him – before ... the dust
returns to the ground it came from ...*
Ecclesiastes 12:6, 7

*M*any men and women try to convince themselves and others that if the ugly parts of life are
overlooked then the world can be regarded as a
kind of heaven. Looked at from one perspective
this world is a beautiful place, but looked at from
another, it is a bad place. It is a world of beautiful
forests, lakes, mountains, seas, yet within every
human heart is a disease called sin which the environment is powerless to eradicate. William Kirk
Kilpatrick made this point: "This healthy mind
works upwards, not downwards. It sees a sun-lamp
and thinks of the sun – not the other way around."

For reading & meditation – Ecclesiastes 12:1-7

JULY 13

It's all so sad

... yet you refuse to come to me to have life.
John 5:40

*F*or one more day we reflect on the fact that this world is not our home. A world such as this, beautiful though it may be, is not good enough to properly be called home. A waiting place – yes. A dwelling place – yes. But not home. Not really. To trivialise the built-in desire we have for heaven and eternity has the same effect on the soul as psychotropic drugs have upon the mind: they dull it and deaden it. Far better to listen to the urge deep within us. I contend that there is something in us all that simply refuses to accept that this world is all there is.

For reading & meditation – John 5:31-47

We have his Word

I am going there to prepare a place for you.
John 14:2

*O*ur human senses are subject to illusions. When we long for something our minds sometimes persuades us that it is available. So how do we know the longing for heaven isn't just a mirage, that it isn't a form of self-delusion? I pointed the young scientist to the words of our text today in which Jesus says: "I am going there to prepare a place for you." We have the best proof possible: Jesus has told us there is a heaven and that a place in it is reserved for the men and women who believe in him. What better evidence do we need than the words of Jesus?

For reading & meditation – John 14:1-14

JULY 15

Memories!

*"I tell you the truth," Jesus answered,
"before Abraham was born, I am!"*
John 8:58

*I*n the text before us today we see quite clearly
that Jesus was aware of his pre-existence. But how
much did he remember of the glories he left
behind? Christ had *some* memories of heaven but
only enough to enable him to fulfil his redemptive mission. He was aware, I believe, to a degree
appropriate to his human condition, of the
atmosphere, the glory and the delights of heaven.
If he had no memories of his pre-existence and
what heaven was like how could he have declared:
"If it were not so, I would have told you" (John
14:2)?

For reading & meditation – John 8:48-58

JULY 16

A human brow

*... he was taken up before their very eyes
and a cloud hid him from their sight.*
Acts 1:9

*A*mong the great doctrines which the Church has debated down the centuries is the doctrine of the impassivity of God. God can't feel, it has been said by some. How can the supreme Being of the universe be troubled by our trifling woes? He can see us, understand us, but he can't enter into our feelings. Well, it would be easier to believe that argument had Jesus not come to earth and worn our flesh. God in Christ has been in our condition, and now our humanity is represented on the throne. Be encouraged to draw near. The Almighty feels as you feel.

For reading & meditation – Acts 1:1-11

JULY 17

Chilly realism

When Jesus saw the crowd ... he gave orders
to cross to the other side of the lake.
Matthew 8:18

*F*rom all that we know of Christ we are com-
pelled to say that in every circumstance he would
tell us the truth. Christ was as much a realist as an
idealist – he never pretended that things were other
than they were. A teacher of the law said: "I will
follow you wherever you go." (v. 19). Christ's
reply was chilly in its realism: "Foxes have holes
and birds ... have nests, but the Son of Man has
nowhere to lay his head." (v. 20). Our Lord went to
great pains to make sure that people understood
him. But he went to great pains also to make sure
that he was not misunderstood.

For reading & meditation – Matthew 8:18-27

JULY 18

Frank and fearless

Jesus turned and said to Peter,
"Get behind me, Satan!"
Matthew 16:23

*A*s Jesus talks about going to Jerusalem and suffering many things at the hands of the elders, chief priests and teachers of the law, Peter remonstrates with him and tries to steer him away from the subject. Peter and the other disciples – let's face it – were somewhat taken up with dreams of imperial power despite our Lord's oft-repeated declaration of the true character of his kingdom. He turns to Peter and says: "Get behind me, Satan! You are a stumbling-block to me; you do not have in mind the things of God, but the things of men." Strong words.

For reading & meditation – Matthew 16:21-28

JULY 19

Candid no less than kind

... a man ran up to him ... "Good teacher,"
he asked, "what must I do to inherit eternal life?"
Mark 10:17

*J*esus looks into the young man's soul and sees
that even though on the surface he may pass the
test of being a commandment-keeper there is
entwined around his heart the love of riches. Now
note what it says in verse 21: "Jesus looked at him
and loved him." But his love is not a sentimental
type of love; it is a love that is strong enough to
confront. With a characteristic thrust of his rapier-
like logic Jesus cuts right to the core issue and
says: "Go, sell everything you have and give to
the poor" (v. 21).

For reading & meditation – Mark 10:17-31

Unthinkable

"No-one has ever gone into heaven except the one who came from heaven – the Son of Man.
John 3:13

Jesus is not just the Christ of candour but also the Christ of compassion. To put it another way: he is not just tough but tender. And the tenderness of his heart would not have allowed him, while in possession of the facts, to conceal them from his followers. He knew full well how men and women longed for some sure word concerning the curtained future; he knew that the question of what lies beyond the grave was something that weighed heavily on their souls; he understood the concern and feelings of their hearts when they contemplated death.

For reading & meditation – John 3:1-16

JULY 21

So it was true!

*No eye has seen, no ear has heard ... what
God has prepared for those who love him ...*
1 Corinthians 2:9

*I*t is said that Professor T.H. Huxley, the famous
agnostic (who, by the way, invented the term
"agnostic" and applied it to himself), reversed his
views prior to his death and came to believe in
God and in future life. As he lay dying (so his
nurse reported) he raised himself on his elbows
and gazed into the distance as if surveying some
invisible scene, then dropped back on his pillow
and murmured: "So it was true! So it was true!"
We who follow Christ need no such revelation to
convince us of the reality of heaven.

For reading & meditation – 1 Corinthians 2:1-16

JULY 22

Keeping heaven in view

For he was looking forward to the city with foundations, whose architect and builder is God.
Hebrews 11:10

*T*he Christians who did most for this world in which we live were those who thought a good deal about the next. It could be argued, that Christians who never allow themselves to think of the world that lies beyond are largely ineffective in this. If the truth be known, most of us go through life with our eyes cast downwards. Those whose eyes are never lifted up to see what lies ahead should not be surprised if they find the things of earth becoming more important to them than heaven, time becoming more important than eternity.

For reading & meditation – Hebrews 11:1-10

JULY 23

Between two gardens

*After he drove the man out, he placed on the
east side of the Garden of Eden cherubim ...*
Genesis 3:24

*G*od is willing to bless his people; indeed he
delights in it. It is not wrong to ask God to resolve
a difficult problem, to heal a serious sickness, or
even work a miracle to help you when in financial
difficulty. I have seen him work in my own life in
all of the ways I have just mentioned, and expect
to see him do the same in the future. That said,
however, our view of the Christian life will be an
unbalanced one if we think that life in Christ means
that we never have to face problems or struggle
with difficulties.

**For reading & meditation – Genesis 3:17-24
and Revelation 22:1-5**

J U L Y   24

A marred joy

... we were harassed at every turn –
conflicts on the outside, fears within.
2 Corinthians 7:5

*I*t is true that because of what Christ did for us
on the cross, which was endorsed by the resurrection and the ascension, we have forgiveness for
our sins (a sure remedy for guilt) and the promise
of the Holy Spirit's help and comfort as we make
our way through this world. But the world we in-
habit is still fallen for all that – it is a world for
which we were not designed. By that I mean that
even in our happiest moments we will experience
a degree of sadness that arises from the fact we
are in an unnatural environment – unnatural in the
sense that a departure from God's intentions is
unnatural.

For reading & meditation – 2 Corinthians 7:1-16

JULY 25

"Struggling well"

*So we fix our eyes not on what is
seen, but on what is unseen.*
2 Corinthians 4:18

*T*he prospect of heaven is something we should always keep before us. It helps us gain a right perspective on everything. Some believe we can have heaven now: "Health and wealth until the day we die." This is nonsense, of course, and quite unscriptural. Yes, God does answer prayer in the way we desire and does work miracles – but not always. Sometimes he lets his people suffer. And it is no good saying the ones who suffer have no faith. That is a cop-out. And a cruel cop-out. The Church needs a theology of suffering to balance its theology of miracles.

For reading & meditation – 2 Corinthians 4:5-18

JULY 26

When rabbits become ferrets

Then Peter stood up with the Eleven,
raised his voice and addressed the crowd ...
Acts 2:14

*T*o the disciples' credit they obeyed the Lord's command to wait in Jerusalem until they were endued with divine power. The men who just a few weeks previously had deserted their Lord were filled with a new courage. And from that day forward the staggering thing is this – not once do we read of the disciples crying out: "If only the Master was with us now." They lived and acted as if the Master was there with them, right at their side. His body was in heaven but the Holy Spirit made his presence universal. It is a mystery of course, but what a *blessed* mystery.

For reading & meditation – Acts 2:1-21

JULY 27

Our travelling Companion

The Lord ... will watch over your life ...
Psalm 121:7

The psalmist says in verse 7: "The Lord will keep you from all harm." The New King James Version says: *"The Lord shall preserve you from all evil."* The promise then is not that we will be kept from hurt but from harm. The two are quite different. Six times in this psalm the Lord is described as the *Keeper* – the One who watches over us. "He may not," as someone has put it, "stop the waves from buffeting us on the outside, but he will stop them from buffeting us on the inside." Each step we take on life's journey we must sing of the fact that though evil may come to us, it will not cause our downfall.

For reading & meditation – Psalm 121:7-8

JULY 28

Living with a tension

*... we ourselves, who have the firstfruits
of the Spirit, groan inwardly ...*
Romans 8:23

*Y*esterday we saw that the whole creation *groans*
But not only does creation groan; we do also. "We
ourselves," says the apostle Paul, "groan inwardly"
as we wait for sin and its effects to be banished
from the universe. Note it is we who are indwelt
by the Spirit who *groan* in this way. Unbelievers
don't share this experience. The Holy Spirit
sensitises our souls to the fact that down here there
is something wrong with almost everything. We
must not allow this to fill us with gloom but we
must accept it nevertheless. It is this groan that
keeps us balanced, knowing that perfection
cannot be brought about by human methods.

For reading & meditation – Romans 8:23-39

JULY 29

You can't improve Paul

For while we are in this tent,
we groan and are burdened ...
2 Corinthians 5:4

Consider with me the matter of living with the tension of joy on the one hand and a groan on the other. Those who sense only the joy of the Christian life and know nothing of the groan live life on a very insensitive level. They go on from day to day thinking only of themselves and are half-deaf to the cries of suffering humanity. They never give a thought to the fact that a large section of the world's population is hungry, and many are even starving. To be blind to this fact (and there are many others) means we will be unable to demonstrate Christ's compassion.

For reading & meditation – 2 Corinthians 5:1-10

JULY 30

The broken snare

*We have escaped like a bird out
of the fowler's snare ...*
Psalm 124:7

*L*ife on this planet is hazardous. We have no idea
what will happen to us in the hours that lie ahead.
We live from one day to the next on the edge of
danger, and sometimes we become caught up in
situations from which there seems just no way out.
Then God comes in glorious deliverance. The trap
is broken and our soul is set free. That doesn't
always happen as quickly as we would like, and it
doesn't always happen the way we would like; it
happens in the way that God sees best. He steps in,
releases the snare and our soul soars, like a bird
set free, to sing at the door of heaven.

For reading & meditation – Psalm 124:6-7

JULY 31

AUGUST

Eager to go

*... I desire to depart and be with Christ ... but it is
more necessary for you that I remain ...*
Philippians 1:23, 24

*T*hroughout the Church's history God's people
have drawn comfort when faced by life's problems
from the promise of heaven. How, for instance,
did slaves in America endure their afflactions? The
"Negro Spirituals", as they are called, give us the
clue. They sang often of the prospect of heaven.
The promise that one day we will be with Jesus in
a perfect world has a powerful effect on our lives
in the present and enables us to cope with difficult situations because it gives us that most
precious of all ingredients – *hope*.

For reading & meditation – Philippians 1:12-26

AUGUST 1

Pay at the toll-bar

... flesh and blood cannot inherit the kingdom of God,
nor does the perishable inherit the imperishable.
1 Corinthians 15:50

*W*hat is the mode of our departure to the heavenly city? It is through death. That is the issue to which we turn our attention now. Death has been described as a toll-bar. At a toll-bar or gate one has to pay "dues". The body in which you and I live is one of the "dues" which has to be paid. It belongs to this earth. We live here in a material world, and the only way we can correspond with our environment is through a material form. But heaven is a spiritual plane and thus this "form" must be left behind. Let it return to the earth from whence it came. It has served its purpose.

For reading & meditation – 1 Corinthians 15:35-58

AUGUST   2

Falling asleep

The child is not dead but asleep.
Mark 5:39

*I*n John 11:11 Jesus refers to the death of Lazarus in this way: "Our friend Lazarus has fallen asleep." There can be absolutely no doubt that Lazarus was, by our definition, dead. Why did Jesus use the word "sleep" when talking about death? Because he saw it in its true perspective – as falling asleep in one world to awaken in another. Of course the world in which one awakens depends on one's relationship to Jesus Christ. Nothing can be more disastrous than to fall asleep in this world and wake up in a world where Christ is not.

For reading & meditation – Mark 5:35-43

Vita! Vita! Vita!

Now this is eternal life: that they may know you, the only true God, and Jesus Christ ...
John 17:3

*T*he early Christians, we are told, carved on the walls of their prisons the words "Vita! Vita! Vita!" Prison walls could not stifle the life that was in them because it was eternal life. Eternal life is a life that death cannot extinguish. By its very nature it is bound to extend beyond the limits of this life. Have you noticed that Jesus never used the word "immortality" when speaking of the future life? He preferred the phrase "eternal life" because that conveyed not merely duration but a quality of life so rich, so abundant, so inexhaustible, that it could not be confined to this present existence.

For reading & meditation – John 17:1-19

AUGUST 4

Everything!

... Christ in you, the hope of glory.
Colossians 1:27

A funeral director once told me he had observed that Christians handle death in a much better way than those who are not Christians. I asked him why he thought that was. After pausing for a few moments he said: "I suppose it's because Christians have a hope beyond the grave." Simple, but profound. Paul makes hope one of the cardinal virtues of the Christian life. The hope the Bible talks about – the hope of life beyond the grave – is more than optimism. It is based on an incontrovertible fact – the resurrection of Jesus from the dead. Jesus not only proclaimed life after death; he demonstrated it.

For reading and meditation – Colossians 1:24-29

AUGUST 5

Like produces like

*While they were stoning him, Stephen
prayed, "Lord Jesus, receive my spirit."*
Acts 7:59

Jesus not only proclaimed life after death – he demonstrated life after death. Some critics have claimed that the disciples stole Jesus' body while the soldiers who were on guard slept. Do the disciples come across in the book of Acts as men who harboured a guilty secret? Do they look like body-snatchers? No, they ploughed their way through persecution, sang their way through prisons and danced their way through death. For what? A hoax? Well hoaxes do not produce hallelujahs nor does body-snatching transform lives. Like produces like.

For reading & meditation – Acts 7:48-60

AUGUST 6

~⚜~

Jesus lives

Because I live, you also will live.
John 14:19

*P*erhaps the most significant reason why Christians do not fear death in the same way that non-Christians fear it is because we know for a fact that Jesus is alive and as our text for today powerfully puts it – because he lives we also will live. Two irreligious men were discussing the resurrection, telling each other why they found it impossible to accept it. Just then an old man whom they knew to be a Christian walked by. Stopping him they enquired: "Sir, tell us why you believe that Jesus Christ rose from the dead?" "Well," said the old man, "one reason is that I was talking to him only a few minutes ago."

For reading & meditation – John 14:15-31

AUGUST 7

Death's main mission

Even though I walk through the valley of the shadow of death, I will fear no evil, for you are with me ...
Psalm 23:4

Many Christians have said to me: "I am not afraid to die but I am anxious about the way in which I will die. Will I be in pain? Will I linger long? Will I be a burden to my loved ones?" All these are legitimate questions and should not be ignored. Whatever the circumstances of our dying, we must never forget that Christ will be with us to the end. But what we must remember above all is this: death has but one mission, and that is to conduct us into the presence of our heavenly Father and to give us a permanent place in the great company of the redeemed.

For reading & meditation – Psalm 23:1-6

AUGUST 8

The Great Divorce

*... wide is the gate and broad is
the road that leads to destruction ...*
Matthew 7:13

C.S. Lewis wrote his little volume entitled *The Great Divorce*. In it he pointed out that we are not living in a world where the roads are the radii of a circle that, if followed long enough, will lead to the centre. Instead (as our Lord told us in the passage before us today), the roads lead in different directions – to heaven or to hell. But being on the wrong road – the broad road – does not inevitably mean that one will finish up in hell. One can choose to turn off it and take the other road – the narrow road – that leads to life and to heaven.

For reading & meditation – Matthew 7:1-13

AUGUST 9

God's great rescue plan

*I am the gate; whoever enters
through me will be saved.*
John 10:9

*O*ne can choose to turn off and take the other
road – the narrow road – that leads to life and to
heaven. The great rescue plan which our Lord Jesus
Christ initiated when he came to this earth enables
us to move from the one road to the other. Our
Lord's great rescue plan accomplished for us on
the cross is the only answer to hell. Because of
this no one goes to hell just because they are bad
and no one goes to heaven just because they are
good. They go to either one of those two places
according to their relationship with Jesus Christ.

For reading & meditation – John 10:1-18

AUGUST   10

Either-or

And if your right hand causes you to sin, cut it off ...
Matthew 5:30

*I*n the passage before us today our Lord presents us with a most solemn challenge. He makes it clear that in this matter of hell it is "either-or". Either we give up our sinful way of life or we face a future in hell. What Jesus is saying in this passage, you see, is this: we must have a disciplined spirit that rejects those things that heaven rejects. I think I can say with certainty that those who get to heaven will not regret for one moment what they abandoned here on earth, no matter how drastic the severance may have been. For the compensations will be beyond all telling.

For reading & meditation – Matthew 5:21-30

AUGUST 11

It has to be surrender

Teach me to do your will, for you are my God ...
Psalm 143:10

I would love with all my heart to be able to build my writing ministry around the idea that all will be saved. However, I have to agree with C.S. Lewis who put the whole issue into a true perspective when he said: "When people say all will be saved my reason retorts: 'Without their will or with it? If I say 'Without their will' I at once perceive a contradiction. How can the supreme voluntary act of self-surrender be involuntary? If I say 'With their will' my reason replies 'How if they will not give in?'"

For reading & meditation – Psalm 143:1-12

AUGUST 12

When heaven would be hell

Outside are the dogs, those who practise magic arts
... everyone who loves and practises falsehood.
Revelation 22:15

*W*hat if a person will not surrender? A certain
man treated his wife (a member of a church I
pastored) as if she was a piece of dirt. "If God
exists," I heard him say, "then he is no different
than I am. He doesn't seem to care two figs for
the universe ... and neither do I." He died, as far as
I can tell, impenitent. The only appropriate des-
tiny for those who stubbornly refuse to come to
Christ is hell. To put them in heaven might be a
worse hell than the one we are talking about. I say
that not with any sense of gloating but out of a
sense of being true to the facts.

For reading & meditation – Revelation 22:12-21

AUGUST 13

Objections to hell

The Lord ... is patient with you, not wanting anyone to perish, but everyone to come to repentance.
2 Peter 3:9

*W*hat are the objections that people raise toward the idea of hell? Take the first version of the argument: God is too good to send people to hell. But in actual fact God doesn't send anyone to hell. They go there of their own accord. Now take the second version: *that a loving heavenly Father will ultimately forgive everyone.* Forgiveness is different from condonation. Forgiveness has to be accepted in order for it to be complete, otherwise it is merely theoretical. A person who does not admit to any guilt will not be able to accept forgiveness.

For reading & meditation – 2 Peter 3:1-18

The clenched fist

*For he himself is our peace, who has ... destroyed the
barrier, the dividing wall of hostility ...*
Ephesians 2:14

*T*he nature with which we are born is not just
disinterested in God; it *hates* him. Some, no matter what, will never yield to the Creator. They prefer enmity to surrender; war to peace. What can
be done with such people? Shouldn't they be left
alone? Well alas, that is what hell is. C.S. Lewis
put it powerfully when he said that there are two
classes of people in the universe: "Those who say
to God, 'Thy will be done' – the saints. And those
to whom God says, 'Thy will be done' – the sinners. " In which class, I wonder, are you?

For reading & meditation – Ephesians 2:11-22

AUGUST 15

Citizens of a new country

But our citizenship is in heaven.
Philippians 3:20

*P*hilippi had the distinction of being a Roman colony, with all the privileges which that brought in the ancient world. But Paul wanted his Philippian readers to understand that they had a higher allegiance – they were citizens of heaven. To be a citizen of heaven means that though during our life here on the earth we obey the laws of the state, pay our taxes, and act honourably and honestly in every circumstance, our supreme loyalty and love lie elsewhere. It is heaven's commands that prevail in our lives, and it is the mind of the King in heaven that we seek to know most of all.

For reading & meditation – Philippians 3:12-21

AUGUST 16

Ambassadors!

We are therefore Christ's ambassadors ...
2 Corinthians 5:20

*I*t is a high privilege to be an ambassador. But there are also dangers associated with the role. According to Lord Templewood in his book *Ambassador on a Special Mission*, one of the dangers an ambassador faces is staying too long in the country to which he has been sent; that is to say, if he does not make frequent visits to his own land, breathe his own native air, reacquaint himself with his native customs and familiarise himself with all that is going on, he can quickly become "denationalised". He must return home frequently, absorb his own atmosphere, renew his strength by contact with his native soil so that he does not lose his orientation.

For reading & meditation – 2 Corinthians 5:11-21

AUGUST 17

Count as dangerous ...

Paul, an apostle of Christ Jesus by the will of God ...
2 Corinthians 1:1

A wise old man told me not long after I had been converted: "The secret of success in the Christian life is to realise that now you have a new nationality. You are Welsh by natural birth but because you have been born again you are now a citizen of heaven. If ever heaven's rules conflict with earth's rules then remember, heaven's rules must take precedence. And remember too," he added, "that the secret of success is prayer. Guard your daily quiet time with God. Speak to him, listen to him, and count as dangerous anything that causes you to lose your links with heaven." You must return whenever you can to your own environment.

For reading & meditation – 2 Corinthians 1:1-11

AUGUST 18

Born into it

"... But I was born a citizen," Paul replied.
Acts 22:28

*T*he apostle Paul was arrested in Jerusalem (see Acts 21:27-36) after unintentionally disturbing the peace, but he proved to be one of the strangest prisoners the commander (the chief captain) had ever taken into custody. Roman citizenship could be acquired in several ways: by birth to Roman parents, on retirement from the army, after having been freed from slavery by a Roman master, as a gift from a Roman general, or by purchase. There is, however, only one way to acquire citizenship in heaven: you have to gain it by birth. Not birth from below, but birth from above.

For reading & meditation – Acts 22:22-29

Not "do" but "done"

For Christ died for sins once for all,
the righteous for the unrighteous
1 Peter 3:16

*S*ome people believe it is possible to attain heavenly citizenship by rigorous moral effort. In other words, you earn it through good works. But as one famous preacher put it – and his use of metaphor is quite brilliant – you cannot work your passage to heaven. A man once said to me: "I never pass up a chance to do someone a good turn. I feel it is always the right thing to do. If there is a heaven then I expect to get into it. It is where I belong." All the good turns in the world will not entitle us to citizenship in heaven. It is commendable to want to serve God, but first there must be reconciliation to him.

For reading & meditation – 1 Peter 3:8-22

A U G U S T   20

More illusions

*... children born not of natural descent, nor of human
decision or a husband's will, but born of God.*
John 1:13

*O*ne other false impression that people have
concerning citizenship in heaven is that it can be
passed on to them from their Christian parents. It
is wonderful to have Christian parents. Godly
parents can do many things: they can dedicate or
christen us, they can teach us the principles of the
faith, they can expose us to the worship of the
Church, but there is one thing they cannot do –
they cannot secure for us a place in heaven. God
will not accept people into heaven on the grounds
of their parents' good works.

For reading & meditation – John 1:1-18

AUGUST 21

The gates of pearl

The twelve gates were twelve pearls,
each gate made of a single pearl.
Revelation 21:21

I have remarked several times before in past
editions of *Every Day with Jesus* that a pearl is a
product of pain. When an oyster is invaded by
something – perhaps a grain of sand – it secretes a
liquid which hardens and then becomes a pearl.
Catch the symbolism of this: the only way into
the city of God is through a gate made of pearl. In
other words, those who enter the city do so
trusting the work that Christ did for them on the
cross. You can't scale those jasper walls. You must
go in through a gate – a gate made of pearl.

For reading & meditation – Revelation 21:1-27

I couldn't find the words

> *You are worthy, our Lord and God,*
> *to receive glory and honour and power ...*
> Revelation 4:11

*T*he book of Revelation, perhaps more than any other book of the Bible, gives us some idea of what heaven is like. In the chapter before us now John shows us that heaven is a place of perpetual praise. All eyes in heaven seem to be directed towards the throne and every creature is vocal in the worship of God and of the Lamb. One of the great delights of earth is when the soul is caught up in praise of God. But in heaven we shall not just be caught up in it; we shall be lost in it. Here our praise is just a rehearsal; there it will be a realisation.

For reading & meditation – Revelation 4:1-11

AUGUST 23

The posture of a servant

As the eyes of slaves look to the hand of
their master ... so our eyes look to the Lord ...
Psalm 123:2

*B*ecause God presented himself to us in Jesus Christ in the form of a servant, we can come perilously close to regarding God as Someone we can order around, Someone we can exploit. God did not become a servant so that he could be exploited but in order that we could bring our lifestyle into line with his. When we look up to him (as opposed to looking down on him) then, at that moment, we are in the posture of a servant. It is important that we understand clearly the relationship that exists between us and the Almighty. He is not here to do our bidding; we are here to do his.

For reading & meditation – Psalm 123:2

A U G U S T   24

Working with
God – endlessly

*... they are before the throne of God and
serve him day and night in his temple ...*
Revelation 7:15

*H*eaven is not just a place of praise; it is a place
of endless service also. There is nothing stagnant
or static about the bliss of heaven. We serve a God
whose creative ability is endless. "My Father is
always at his work," Jesus said (John 5:17). Some
take that to refer to God's work in redemption and
say that when that work is complete he will stop.
Yet I cannot believe God will ever be unemployed
or go into retirement. He will be engaged in
creative and endless efforts and we, the church,
will be at his side, working with him.

For reading & meditation – Revelation 7:1-17

AUGUST 25

In the thick of things

*The throne of God and of the Lamb will be
in the city, and his servants will serve him.*
Revelation 22:3

*T*homas Carlyle, the writer, pictured God as sitting on a throne in eternity "doing nothing". That is not the way I imagine him. I see him as a Worker who will involve his children in working with him in the kind of work that is purposeful and satisfying. Henry Ward Beecher, the famous American preacher remarked: "I suppose one day they will bring me out here and leave me, but I won't stay here. I'll be somewhere right in the thick of things, working for God."

For reading & meditation – Revelation 22:1-11

Joy – the serious business

... you will fill me with joy in your presence.
Acts 2:28

*A*s well as being a place of praise and service heaven is a place of indescribable joy. C.S. Lewis wrote in one of his books: "Joy is the serious business of heaven." Think how often heaven and joy are linked together in the New Testament. Jesus said on one occasion: "There is joy before the angels of God over one sinner who repents" (Luke 15:10, RSV). And when telling the Parable of the Talents he promised that those who use their talents and multiply them will hear the Master say: "Enter into the joy of your master" (Matt. 25:21, RSV).

For reading & meditation – Acts 2:22-28

AUGUST   27

Gales of laughter

Sarah said, "God has brought me laughter ..."
Genesis 21:6

A word that is associated with joy is laughter. Frequently I have been asked: Will there be laughter in heaven? Personally, I have no doubt about it. The God who made Sarah to laugh, does he not laugh himself? I believe that gales of laughter will echo from the redeemed, and we shall discover, I think, that however much we have laughed down here on earth it will be as nothing compared to the laughter of heaven. Scripture hints that there is laughter and joy in the heart of God. Why only hints? If the Lord veils his glory lest it be too bright for mortal eyes then might he not also veil his joy?

For reading & meditation – Genesis 21:1-7

AUGUST 28

No more

*... but when perfection comes,
the imperfect disappears.*
1 Corinthians 13:10

*T*here will be no more death, the apostle John
says, no more crying, no more sorrow, no more
pain, no longer any curse, no more night, and so
on. The reason for heaven's perfection is that sin,
which is the cause of all imperfection, has no place
or part in that eternal realm. But is it likely that
sin will again break out in heaven? It did once
with Lucifer. Might not someone mar its beauty
and harmony by a collision of their will with
God's? Have no fear. Sin will not only be impossible but unthinkable. As unthinkable for us as it
will be for the Saviour to whom we will be joined.

For reading & meditation – 1 Corinthians 13:1-13

AUGUST 29

A new name!

I will also give him ... a new name ...
known only to him who receives it.
Revelation 2:17

The name Jacob stood for supplanter; the name
Jesus for Saviour. What is more personal to us than
our names? We are easily offended when people
refer to us as numbers. "I am not a number, I am a
person with a name," we say. It seems, however,
that the new name we will be given in heaven will
be a secret between God and each one of us. What
can we take this secrecy to mean? That every one
of us will relate to God in a way that is personal.
You will be part of a great host but it will also be
as if it were just you and your Father in heaven.

For reading & meditation – Revelation 2:12-17

~·//·~

Homeward bound

*For here we do not have an enduring city,
but we are looking for the city that is to come.*
Hebrews 13:14

*T*wo ships passed each other – one a large sailing
ship, the other a small steamer. The captain of the
little steamer picked up his megaphone and hailed
the great sailing ship: "Who are you?" In response
a strong voice boomed out from the megaphone
on the other ship: "I am the Begun of Bengal, 124
days out of Canton, having delivered perfumes and
spices to many ports of the world, and now, home-
ward bound." As Christians we can make a similar claim. We are happily engaged in dropping off
the perfume of heaven on our way through this
world, but our greatest joy is this: *we are home-
ward bound.*

For reading & meditation – Hebrews 13:7-21

AUGUST 31

SEPTEMBER

Blessed obsession!

*May I never boast except in the
cross of our Lord Jesus Christ ...*
Galatians 6:14

*F*or weeks and months after I was converted I was overwhelmed by the cross. That was the theme the evangelist was expounding the night I gave my heart and life to Christ. The redemptive, glorious mystery of it took hold of me and for a long while afterwards I wondered why anyone should preach about anything except the cross. Now fifty years later my inmost being still glows when I think or talk about the cross. On one occasion I was even accused of being obsessed with it. Blessed obsession! It is here that we see into the depth of things, here the heart of the universe shows itself.

For reading & meditation – Galatians 6:1-18

SEPTEMBER 1

A sacrificial Head

... God ... loved us and sent his Son
as an atoning sacrifice for our sins.
1 John 4:10

*S*ome creatures at the bottom end of the scale feed on their young. But as we rise higher in the scale of life we find parent animals sacrificing themselves for the sake of their offspring. When we come to humankind we find beings who will not only sacrifice themselves for their young but will at times sacrifice themselves for someone whom they do not even know. Here life rises to its most elevated form. The highest being is the one who is willing to sacrifice most for other. When we come to God, we would expect to find the most highly developed expression of sacrificial love.

For reading & meditation – Matthew 27:32-44

SEPTEMBER 2

The infallible law

Will not the Judge of all the earth do right?
Genesis 18:25

*T*he spirit of self sacrifice is built into us by divine design. Within us there is a sense of justice, a justice which causes us to feel it is right to save even at a cost to oneself. If this "infallible law", as some psychologists describe it, remains true up through the scale of being but reverses itself when it gets to God, then laws are meaningless and the universe is without a Head. But on the other hand, if this law holds good from the very lowest to the very highest, as the sacrificial spirit of the cross implies, then the universe is whole, laws are not enigmas and God is not a disappointment.

For reading & meditation – Genesis 18:16-33

The nature of love

Does he who implanted the ear not hear?
Does he who formed the eye not see?
Psalm 94:9

*I*t is the nature of love universally to insinuate itself into the sorrows and sins of the one it loves and make them its very own. In a home where pure love meets sin or wrongdoing in the one who is loved, a cross of pain is set up, inevitably, at the point where the two meet. "All love," says one writer, "has the doom of bleeding upon it as long as there is sin in the loved one. And that love, when it meets the sin, soon crimsons into suffering." Is it surprising then to discover that at the point where God's love and our sin meet a cross has been set up? It could not be otherwise, love being what it is.

For reading & meditation – Psalm 94:1-23

SEPTEMBER 4

The eternal cross

Who shall separate us from the love of Christ?
Romans 8:35

*A*n overseas student once said to me: "I do no
understand what God is like. I see glimpses of him
here and there. But they are all so fleeting. I can'
pin down his real nature." I told him about the
cross – God's greatest self-revelation. "Ah, I see i
now," he said. "God's real nature is love. The cross
proves it." Later he remarked: "Fancy having to
cross the sea in order to see the cross." No one
need cross a sea to see the cross, but if it were
necessary, the revelation would be more than worth
the effort.

For reading & meditation – Romans 8:31-39

The cross – central

For I resolved to know nothing while I was with you except Jesus Christ and him crucified.
1 Corinthians 2:2

*A*s a young Christian I was taught that no one can come to Christ except through the cross and no one can get to know Christ except through the cross. Time and time again when I hear on television or read in some newspaper or magazine the ridiculous statement that "all religions are the same" my mind runs involuntarily to Calvary. No other religion has a cross. It is absolutely unique. The time has come, I believe, to put the cross back where it belongs; not on the periphery but at the centre of our faith. No cross – no Christianity. It is as stark and as simple as that.

For reading & meditation – 1 Corinthians 2:1-16

SEPTEMBER 6

The glorious cross

For the message of the cross is foolishness to those who are perishing, but to us ... it is the power of God.
1 Corinthians 1:18

*T*heologians have devised a number of theories in their attempt to explain the mystery of the cross, but no theory it seems to me is big enough to fit the facts. Just as Jesus broke the bars of death and stepped beyond the tomb, so the fact of Jesus dying seems to transcend all statements and theories. They are attempts to tell the untellable, to speak the unspeakable. To see the cross in all its glory we must gaze at it from different vantage points. Looked at from one viewpoint it is wonderful, but looked at from a number of viewpoints it is more than wonderful. It is sublime.

For reading & meditation – 1 Corinthians 1:10-25

SEPTEMBER   7

The cross – a kaleidoscope

*... the Lamb that was slain
from the creation of the world.*
Revelation 13:8

*W*e can't begin to understand the cross until we see it in a cosmic and eternal setting. The crucifixion of Christ was not merely an earthly affair conducted clandestinely in an obscure corner of the Roman Empire. It spans all time and transcends all history. Jesus was the Lamb slain from the creation of the world. As one theologian put it: "There was a cross in the heart of God before there was ever one planted on the green hill outside Jerusalem." Let the thought thrill you – God had a Lamb before he had a man!

For reading & meditation – Revelation 13:1-9

Redemption anticipated

*He is the image of the invisible
God, the firstborn over all creation.*
Colossians 1:15

*T*oday we ask ourselves: Why was it necessary
for the Lamb to be slain from the creation of the
world? When God created the world and laid down
the broad beams that formed the universe he
foresaw that evil would enter his creation and
prepared for it by building into it a cross. By
creating the universe and endowing creatures with
the dangerous gift of free will God brought into
existence the conditions in which evil became a
possibility. In designing the universe, however,
God made sure that the possibility of sin was met
by the possibility of redemption.

For reading & meditation – Colossians 1:15-23

SEPTEMBER 9

Part of the structure

*... without the shedding of
blood there is no forgiveness.*
Hebrews 9:22

Dr Albert Schweitzer may have been a humanitarian with a brilliant mind but he was in a spiritual fog when it came to the cross. "Jesus," he said, "expected the kingdom to come at Jerusalem. And when it didn't he died on the cross of a broken heart, crying, 'My God, my God, why hast thou forsaken me?' But in dying he left an ethic of love." Those who see the cross as an afterthought fail to understand its meaning. The cross is a forethought — a fact worked into the texture of creation. It is, as someone put it, the groundplan of the universe. It comes out of the universe because it was built into the universe.

For reading & meditation– Hebrews 9:11-28

SEPTEMBER   10

A cruciform cosmos

"He saved others," they said,
"but he can't save himself!"
Matthew 27:42

*F*iremen will go into a burning building and risk their own lives in order to save a stranger in distress and endanger his own life because something deep within him prompts him to do so. What is this "something"? It is, in my view, the law of self-sacrifice which runs like a scarlet thread through history. Those who save others cannot save themselves trouble, pain, suffering, even death. Where does this desire to save others at the cost of one's own life come from? Is it, perhaps, explainable by the fact that we are made in the image of God – a God who gave himself up for others?

For reading & meditation – Matthew 27:32-44

SEPTEMBER 11

The cross – inherent

And being in anguish, he prayed more earnestly ...
Luke 22:44

*N*ot long ago I visited Winchester Cathedral with a friend. As we gazed around he looked up and pointed to the rood-screen and said: "There's a cross up there." Then he pointed to the floor of the cathedral and said: "And there's a cross down here." Like so many ancient places of worship the whole cathedral is a cross – it is a cruciform building. Chancel and nave for the upright, the two transepts for the cross-beam. The cross is inherent in life. It is life's foundation, not an incongruity. Our Saviour, when he died at Golgotha, focused in a moment of time a fact which is in reality timeless. On that first Good Friday the Lamb slain from the creation of the world was *seen* slain.

For reading & meditation – Luke 22:39-46

SEPTEMBER   12

As the flash of a volcano

He was chosen before the creation of the world, but was revealed in these last times ...
1 Peter 1:20

*T*he cross was in the heart of God aeons before it stood stark on the crest of the hill of Calvary, and the supreme crisis of the passion which short-sightedly we assume took place in Gethsemane may have been suffered by our Lord before time began. "As the flash of a volcano discloses for a few hours the elemental fires at the earth's centre," wrote the theologian Dinsmore, "so the light of Calvary was the bursting forth through historical conditions of the very nature of the Everlasting."

For reading & meditation – 1 Peter 1:13-25

SEPTEMBER 13

"It could not be otherwise"

Concerning this salvation, the prophets ...
searched intently and with the greatest care ...
1 Peter 1:10

*F*rom the very beginning of the Scriptures we
catch sight of what we might call the prophetic
cross. Dr A.C. Dixon in his book *The Glories of
the Cross* likens the Bible to a sunrise. "It is interesting," he says, "to stand on a hill top and watch the
coming dawn; first, the grey streaks in the East,
and then the brighter light until the full-orbed sun
arises. *There is a sunrise with its dawn like that in
the Old Testament Scriptures*." Just as the cross is
written into the cosmos so is it written also into
almost every page of the Old Testament. It could
not be otherwise.

For reading & meditation – 1 Peter 1:1-12

SEPTEMBER 14

Foresight and feeling

For prophecy never had its origin in the will of man, but men spoke from God as they were carried along by the Holy Spirit.
2 Peter 1:21

I remember that when I first began to study the Bible I found it incredible that hundreds of years before Christ died on the cross people were predicting the event in fine detail. Someone has computed that the likelihood of the Old Testament prophecies concerning Christ's death coming true by chance is one in five billion. Yet they did – to the very letter. The Old Testament writers who focus on the cross describe our Lord's sufferings not from without but from within.

For reading & meditation – 2 Peter 1:12-21

SEPTEMBER 15

The Psalm of Sobs

My God, my God, why have you forsaken me?
Psalm 22:1

Sometimes it seems the Old Testament is like a voice and the New Testament like the echo. The Old Testament predicts and the New Testament records. Look with me at a few of these correspondences. The mockery spoken of in Psalm 22 verse 7 is echoed by the derision of the priests in Matthew 27:39. The dividing of the clothing in verse 18 is answered by the act of the soldiers referred to in John 19:23. And the powerful verses (vv. 14-17) in which the psalmist describes such deep suffering are echoed by every one of the Gospel writers. A genuine personal experience of the psalmist is used by the Holy Spirit to provide him with a foreshadowing of Christ's experience.

For reading & meditation – Psalm 22:1-18

SEPTEMBER 16

A most moving passage

But he was pierced for our transgressions,
he was crushed for our iniquities ...
Isaiah 53:5

*I*saiah 53 is one of the most moving passages in the Old Testament. Several times in this chapter we are told the Messiah suffers in order to take away our sins. Take these for example. (1) He is pierced for our transgressions. (2) He was crushed for our iniquities. (3) The Lord laid on him the iniquity of us all. (4) By oppression and judgment he was taken away. (5) His life was made an offering for sin. (6) He will bear their iniquities. (7) He bore the sin of many. How marvellously the words of Isaiah came to be fulfilled can be seen not only by an examination of the Gospels but of other New Testament writings also.

For reading & meditation – Isaiah 53:1-12

SEPTEMBER 17

Death by a broken heart

Scorn has broken my heart
and has left me helpless ...
Psalm 69:20

"*D*eath from a broken heart," says Hodgin in his classic *Christ in all the Scriptures* "is very rare." The loud cry, the fact of death coming so soon, the effect of the spear-thrust, all point towards this being indeed the cause of our Lord's death." When one of the soldiers approached Jesus to accelerate his death by breaking his legs he found that Jesus was already dead. The soldier then pierced his side, which caused a gush of blood and water. The bearing of our sins, and the hiding of the Father's face on account of it, literally broke his heart.

For reading & meditation – Psalm 69:1-21

SEPTEMBER 18

The event of eternity

The Son of Man will go just as it is written about him.
Matthew 26:24

I heard one professor of Old Testament studies say that if the New Testament were somehow to be taken away from us and all record of it removed (a tragedy we cannot envisage), it would almost be possible to reconstruct the closing scenes in the drama of Christ's life from the relevant prophetic passages in the Old Testament. So much of the Old Testament is prophetic, and a good deal of that prophecy focuses on the coming of Christ and his death on the cross. The shadow of the cross is not only on creation; it is cast over the Old Testament also. The cross is *the* event of eternity.

For reading & meditation – Matthew 26:17-30

SEPTEMBER 19

The divine secret

*... he was filled with wisdom, and
the grace of God was upon him.*
Luke 2:40

*W*hen and how did our Lord first understand that he was the promised Messiah? Was it something that came to him suddenly? Or did it dawn on him gradually over weeks, or months, or even years? My own view is that in the period referred to in our text today (between his consecration as a baby and his Bar Mitzvah at the age of thirteen) as he read, prayed and pondered the Old Testament Scriptures, gradually the Holy Spirit revealed to him that he was the One of whom the prophets spoke. What a momentous time that must have been in his young life.

For reading & meditation – Luke 2:21-40

SEPTEMBER 20

The shadow of death

But his mother treasured all these things in her heart.
Luke 2:51

*H*olman Hunt in his beautiful painting *The Shadow of Death* depicts the inside of the carpenter's shop in Nazareth and has Jesus stripped to his waist. He lifts his hands towards heaven as if stretching to relieve his aching arms. On the wall is a tool rack giving the impression of a horizontal bar, to which, in the painting, his hands appear to be nailed. Even the tools themselves are a grim reminder of the hammer and nails used in Christ's crucifixion. The idea may be fanciful but nevertheless it is true theologically. The shadow of the cross was over Jesus from his earliest years.

For reading & meditation – Luke 2:41-52

SEPTEMBER   21

The Messianic secret

He then began to teach them that the
Son of Man must suffer many things ...
and that he must be killed ...
Mark 8:31

Jesus did not want his Messianic role to be revealed until his character had been more clearly established and second, he wanted to carefully unfold the revelation *himself*. Jesus began to fill in some of the details concerning his death: he would be rejected by the elders, chief priests and teachers of the law, and would be killed but after three days rise again. When Peter heard this he was horrified and sharply rebuked Jesus. But Jesus, in turn, vehemently rebuked Peter. He had come into the world to die.

For reading & meditation – Mark 8:27-33

SEPTEMBER 22

When afraid – avoid

*But they did not understand what he meant
and were afraid to ask him about it.*
Mark 9:32

Jesus gives the disciples a little more information in that he makes plain that he would be betrayed into the hands of men – the first hint of the betrayal. The words he used are similar to those of the first prediction, but this time we are informed the disciples did not understand the meaning of what he said and were afraid to question him. We are always afraid when things fail to go the way we think they should. Fear becomes a defence that helps us avoid the hard facts of reality. To avoid being disturbed the disciples were afraid to ask Jesus any further questions.

For reading & meditation – Mark 9:14-32

SEPTEMBER 23

Determined to die

They were on their way up to Jerusalem ...
and the disciples were astonished, while
those who followed were afraid.
Mark 10:32

*J*esus did not relish death (as is made plain by his struggle in the Garden of Gethsemane), but such was his commitment to doing his Father's will that he put aside his own feelings. John Stott says of our Lord's threefold repetition of the passion prediction found in Mark's Gospel that "it is Mark's way of preparing his readers, as Jesus deliberately prepared the Twelve, for the terrible events that would take place." He was determined to die. Not because of a death-wish but out of a desire to serve the Father's purposes.

For reading & meditation – Mark 10:32-45

SEPTEMBER 24

Uppermost in his mind

... Jesus ... looked towards heaven and
prayed: "Father, the time has come."
John 17:1

*T*hough Jesus saw his teaching as important, his example as crucial, and his miracles as an essential part of his ministry, none of these dominated his mind as did the thought of going to the cross. What seemed to be uppermost in his thoughts was not so much his life, but the giving of his life. This, as our text for today puts it, was the "time" (or "hour") for which he had come into the world. He was determined to fulfil what was predicted of him no matter how painful or difficult it would be. For he had come, as one Scripture tells us, "to seek and to save what was lost" (Luke 19:10).

For reading & meditation – John 17:1–19

SEPTEMBER 25

A most incongruous thing

When they came to the place called the
Skull, there they crucified him ...
Luke 23:33

*T*he Biblical account of the crucifixion is as stark as the cross itself. There are few detailed descriptions of crucifixion recorded in history. Most writers seem to have avoided the subject, and we can well understand why. Crucifixion was one of the most barbarous and horrifying forms of execution, in which a living, breathing man was fastened to some timbers and allowed to hang there for days. This form of torture was devised to produce the maximum amount of pain over the longest period of time. How incongruous it seems that our Lord should die such a death.

For reading & meditation – Luke 23:26-43

SEPTEMBER 26

The horrors of crucifixion

"What shall I do, then, with Jesus
who is called Christ?" Pilate asked.
They all answered, "Crucify him!".
Matthew 27:22

*C*rucifixion was the most dreadful method of administering the death penalty. So brutal and humiliating was it that only the worst class of criminals was executed in this way. Cicero, the Roman philosopher, described it as "a most cruel and disgusting punishment". Later he declared: "The very word 'cross' should be far removed not only from the person of a Roman citizen, but from his thoughts, his eyes and his ears." That our Lord should be subjected to death on a cross is so shocking that the human mind can scarely comprehend it.

For reading & meditation – Matthew 27:11-26

SEPTEMBER 27

Three types of cross

Above his head they placed the
written charge against him ...
Matthew 27:37

 ifferent types of crosses were used by the
Romans. On which of these was our Lord nailed?
"Above his head they placed the written charge
against him." Note the words "above his head".
That superscription could not have been fixed there
unless the gibbet was constructed in the way it is
traditionally depicted – as a crossbeam and an
upright post. Exposure, fever, hunger, shock and
exhaustion were usually the immediate causes of
death. No wonder people speak of Christ's death
on the cross as a tragedy. Why should such a bad
thing happen to such a good person?

For reading & meditation – Matthew 27:32-44

SEPTEMBER   28

Nothing more wonderful

*Christ redeemed us from the curse of
the law by becoming a curse for us ...*
Galatians 3:13

*T*he sinner who would be condemned to death
by the law can now be alive to God. Free from the
curse he is open to the blessing of God that comes
through Christ. This is a truth that I find many
Christians pass over too quickly. They say it is too
difficult to understand. It simply means that Christ,
by his atoning sacrifice on the cross, has borne
our shame and, in bearing that shame, has put to
death the demands of the law over us. We died in
him and because he lives we live in him. Nothing
in heaven or earth is more wonderful. Nothing!

For reading & meditation – Galatians 3:1-14

SEPTEMBER   29

He suffered

He had Jesus flogged, and
handed him over to be crucified.
Mark 15:15

*T*he Apostles' Creed puts it: "He suffered under Pontius Pilate." *Suffered!* The account of our Lord's death is not a sentimental tale spun on the loom of fantasy; it is a record of hard, terrible reality. Jesus, we should remember, did not die in a cathedral surrounded by choristers but was suspended above the earth and left limp and bleeding, a public spectacle on a hill outside a city wall. The glory of the cross lies in its starkness. A cross was a symbol of failure but Christ turned it into a symbol of achievement. Now the cross conveys to the world not *its* message but *his*.

For reading & meditation – Mark 15:1-15

SEPTEMBER 30

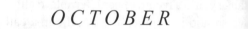

OCTOBER

The sublime paradox

*Did not the Christ have to suffer
these things and then enter his glory?*
Luke 24:26

*G*od came to earth in the form of a man and was whipped, spat upon, pierced with nails and hung up naked for everyone to jeer at. Looked at in this way the crucifixion is almost too shocking for us to comprehend it. It is, as someone described it, "the great incongruity". But that is only half of the story. In the midst of "the great incongruity" there is a great congruity too. The cross is a sublime paradox. An enormous incongruity; a lovely congruity. The worst thing the world has ever done; the best thing heaven has ever done. A great crime; a great love.

For reading & meditation – Luke 24:13-32

OCTOBER 1

The unavoidable cross

*For Christ died for sins once for all, the righteous
for the unrighteous, to bring you to God.*
1 Peter 3:18

One of the great tragedies of the human race is that we fail to realise the sinfulness of sin. We tend to call our sins "mistakes", "slips", "failures" or "indiscretions". And when we do use the word "sin" we use it lightly and with no sense of culpability. What is sin? It is acting independently of God, treating him as if he didn't exist, relegating the great Creator of the universe to irrelevance. Sin, when taken to its nth degree, would, if it could, push God out of the very universe he made. This is what was attempted at Calvary. Sin is a foul blot in God's universe and it takes the cross to make us realise what it is really like.

For reading & meditation – 1 Peter 3:8-22

OCTOBER 2

The ugliness of sin

*... God ... made us alive with Christ even
when we were dead in transgressions ...*
Ephesians 2:4,5

*W*e sometimes think that Christ was put to death
by the serious sins of the religious leaders of his
day, but it was by the accumulation of what we
sometimes call "little sins" as well. Things like
gossip, slander, greed, bigotry, fear were all present
at Calvary. We might never have known the deadly
nature of sin (all sins – little or big) unless it had
been placarded before our eyes. In the light of the
cross it is impossible to discuss sin academically.
For there it is seen for what it is. Think about this
as you go about your duties this day: every one of
us has been guilty of the sins that nailed Christ to
his cross.

For reading & meditation – Ephesians 2:1-10

OCTOBER 3

No cross – no salvation

*They spoke about his departure, which he was
about to bring to fulfilment at Jerusalem.*
Luke 9:31

Sin always has a price and somebody must pay.
The punishment of sin is death, and it was necessary for someone to bear the piled-up debt of the
human race – someone who was not only willing
but worthy. The debt created by our sin was met
by Jesus. What no other man could do this man
did. By his death on the cross he paid for our sin
in such a way that he bore it all away. He fought
sin and defeated it. Let there be no serious talk
about the cross being unnecessary. Perhaps the
shortest answer to that suggestion is this: if the
cross was unnecessary it would never have been.

For reading & meditation – Luke 9:28-36

OCTOBER 4

Why such violence?

With a loud cry, Jesus breathed his last.
Mark 15:37

*W*hy couldn't Christ have been put to death suddenly with the minimum of pain or distress? I have always been indebted to Dr W.E. Sangster for his explanations as to why Christ's death had to be violent. This is how he put it: "Could he (Christ) have exposed sin in all its foul horror if he had died in his bed ... or by accident? Only a violent death could have exposed sin in the way sin so sorely needed exposing." What it amounts to is this: Christ had to die to save us and he had to die by way of the cross. I don't know about you, but I just can't put into words the gratitude I feel to my Saviour for submitting to such a death on my behalf.

For reading & meditation – Mark 15:21-39

OCTOBER 5

I have suffered too!

*... Put your finger here; see my hands. Reach out
your hand and put it into my side.*
John 20:27

Jesus says to Thomas: "Behold the marks of my
crucifixion." This is how our Lord deals with us
too. He stands in front of us and says: "Look at
these hands; they were nailed to a tree. I know
how you feel. Let me enter into your sorrows." As
a preacher of the gospel I have been grateful on
hundreds of occasions when confronted by someone writhing in deep mental anguish that I have a
crucified Saviour I can talk about. More eloquently
than any words, those pierced hands say: "I have
suffered too!"

For reading & meditation – John 20:24-31

OCTOBER 6

At-one

God presented him as a sacrifice of atonement,
through faith in his blood.
Romans 3:25

*W*illiam Tyndale, when translating the New Testament into English, found the language of his day woefully inadequate to express the richness of the Greek. Particularly baffling was the word which Paul used to express the redeeming work of Christ on the cross – *katallage*. So joining together the simple words "at" and "one" he gave us the word "atonement", which has passed into theological currency. Its etymology, therefore, provides us with the clue to its meaning – the bringing together of God and man so that the two parties who were once separated by sin are now *at one*.

For reading & meditation – Romans 3:21-31

OCTOBER 7

Jesus is the Atonement!

... he had to be made like his brothers in
every way ... that he might make
atonement for the sins of the people.
Hebrews 2:17

*B*ecause Jesus is God and man he is both human
and divine. This is the whole point of the
incarnation – God took on human flesh and thus
combined the two natures in one Person. Those
who do not believe in the virgin birth of Christ
will certainly not believe in the atoning death of
Christ for the one depends on the other. If Jesus
had not joined himself to us in the incarnation then
he would not have been able to join us to God in
the atonement. "A Saviour who is not quite God,"
said Bishop Handley Moule, "is a like a bridge
broken at the farther end." He is right.

For reading & meditation – Hebrews 2:5-18

OCTOBER 8

He who had no sin ...

God made him who had no sin to be sin for us ...
2 Corinthians 5:21

*T*heologians use the word passion to describe the events connected with the crucifixion and death of our Lord, and it is on his passion that we are focusing now. No verse in the whole of the New Testament puts the truth of the atonement more clearly than the one before us today: "God made him who had no sin to be sin for us ..." How can anybody be made sin for someone else? How can the innocent suffer for the guilty? I don't know. And neither does anyone else. It is a mystery. But this I know: He who had no sin was made sin on our behalf. This goes beyond our understanding, but we can experience the benefits even though we do not understand it.

For reading & meditation – 2 Corinthians 5:11-21

OCTOBER 9

"Fellow lepers!"

He himself bore our sins in his body on the tree ...
1 Peter 2:24

*F*ather Damien, a missionary, was the only healthy man on an island of lepers. One morning he splashed boiling water on to his bare foot. He felt nothing. Then the truth dawned on him. One of the signs of leprosy is immunity to pain. He was a leper himself! Most men would have been devastated but do you know what Father Damien did? He rang the church bell to summon everyone to the building. When all had gathered he leapt into the pulpit, stretched out his arms and said: "Fellow lepers." From that moment on his words gained greater credibility. The people who heard him speak all agreed: "He is one of us." This story gives a clear illustration of Jesus' atonement.

For reading & meditation – 1 Peter 2:13-25

OCTOBER 10

A good perspective

... how much more, having been reconciled,
shall we be saved through his life!
Romans 5:10

*W*ith the best will in the world, you and I could never be righteous like Jesus. As well ask us to write a play like Shakespeare, paint pictures like Raphael or compose music like Beethoven. We just couldn't do it. The amazing fact, however, is this: ordinary folk like you and me can live like Jesus Christ – righteously – because he not only imputes his righteousness to us through the cross but imparts it by coming and living in us. Christianity is the only religion in the world whose Founder rose from the dead and came back to live his life in and through his followers.

For reading & meditation – Romans 5:1-11

OCTOBER 11

Unified personalities

*... he who raised Christ from the dead will also give
life to your mortal bodies through his Spirit ...*
Romans 8:11

*H*ave you ever considered what results from the
presence of Christ in our hearts? Many things, of
course, but consider just one: his presence unifies
our personalities. As people we are terribly
complicated. One psychologist said: "We are not
the same person from one minute to the other."
Our moods and thoughts are constantly changing.
When Jesus Christ comes into the heart, however,
all this is changed. The multiple personality is
unified. Then we can say with the apostle Paul: "I
no longer live, but Christ lives in me" (Gal. 2:20).
And how!

**For reading & meditation – Romans 7:14-25;
8:1-11**

OCTOBER 12

Two words – two worlds

Come and see the place where he lay.
Matthew 28:6

*W*e see in the passage before us today that Mary was surprised when she found the tomb empty. But imagine the effect upon her and the ages if the Lord still lay there. As a poet put it:

O, the anguish of Mary!
O, the depth of despair!
Had she gone to the tomb,
And the dead Lord was there.

How wonderful it is that we do not have to say "Come and see the place where he *lies*," but "Come and see the place where he *lay*." Two different words – two different worlds. Hallelujah!

For reading & meditation – Matthew 28:1-15

OCTOBER 13

Horizons

... his Son ... was declared with power to be the Son of God, by his resurrection from the dead ...
Romans 1:3,4

*C*hrist was "declared with power to be the Son of God." The word "declared" in the Greek comes from the verb horizo and is the term from which we get the word "horizon". The resurrection of our Lord has given a completely new horizon to the gospel. Christ, whose bodily presence occupied only a few cubic feet in Palestine prior to the resurrection, became on Easter Day the One who was no longer limited, but unlimited. He rose from the dead to fill all space and all time. Our Lord, on that glorious resurrection morning, pushed back all horizons, and through his rising from the dead has opened up for us the unending vistas of eternity.

For reading & meditation – Romans 1:1-7

OCTOBER 14

Power from a tomb!

*I want to know Christ and the
power of his resurrection ...*
Philippians 3:10

*P*ower from the tomb means this: the energy that was focused in bringing Christ back from the dead is available to you and me – to save us, sanctify us and get us ready for heaven. All the forces of earth conspired to keep Christ in the grave. They put a large stone over the mouth of his grave, sealed it with a Roman seal, and posted a guard to stop anyone moving it. But the power that was *in* the tomb was greater than any power that was *without*. One writer worded it like this: "On the day of resurrection God took the seal from off the tomb and put it on the gospel."

For reading & meditation – Philippians 3:1-11

OCTOBER 15

Crucified afresh

*... to their loss they are crucifying
the Son of God all over again ...*
Hebrews 6:6

I think it is true to say that few believers would openly deny Christ and pledge to have nothing more to do with him. But do we realise that to profess to be one of his followers and yet refuse to live as he commanded is in itself a form of denial? I speak metaphorically, of course, but the Saviour bleeds again when we choose not to obey his commands and act in a way that brings dishonour to his Name. Our Lord's pain did not end when he expired on the cross. The suffering of the cross continues every time we put our own interests before his.

For reading & meditation – Hebrews 6:1-12

OCTOBER 16

Again he bleeds

*They divided my garments among
them and cast lots for my clothing.*
John 19:24

A certain church building had been padlocked
and sealed because two factions in the church had
quarrelled. Both factions were denied the use of
the building because of violence that erupted. The
two factions then attempted to settle the matter of
the building's ownership by going to court. As
Christ hung dying upon the cross some soldiers
sat around and cast lots for his clothes. Casting
lots for his clothes and gambling over court deci-
sions for possession of property – is there any
difference? In my opinion, little or none! *Again
he bleeds.*

For reading & meditation – John 19:16-24

OCTOBER 17

Not on speaking terms

First go and be reconciled to your brother ...
Matthew 5:24

*L*et us have done with thinking that we have to walk away from the faith and deny we ever had anything to do with Christ in order to crucify him afresh. We do so also when we stubbornly refuse to follow the principles he has laid out for us in his Word – principles such as forgiveness and reconciliation, for example. It is unrealistic to expect that Christians will never fall out with one another, but we need not and must not allow that situation to remain. We are to work at being reconciled to one another. When we fail to follow directives then, believe me, the suffering of the cross continues. Our Saviour is in pain.

For reading & meditation – Matthew 5:17-26

OCTOBER 18

Paul's pain – Christ's pain

> *... I fill up in my flesh what is still
> lacking in regard to Christ's afflictions ...*
> Colossians 1:24

*W*hat was lacking in Christ's afflictions? Nothing, if we are talking about the price Christ paid for our redemption on the cross. There is no deficiency in the atoning work of Christ. No one can, or need, add to his finished and perfect work. Rather, Paul was referring to the afflictions he was called to bear "for the sake of ... the church" when presenting the gospel. Dr E. Stanley Jones gave an intriguing interpretation of this verse. He said that when Paul was suffering "for the sake of the Church", Christ, too, was suffering in Paul's sufferings. In other words, Paul's pain was Christ's pain.

For reading & meditation – Colossians 1:24-29

OCTOBER   19

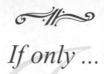

If only ...

*... he will answer, "The wounds I was
given at the house of my friends."*
Zechariah 13:6

*I*n one country I visited I saw a sign outside a
church that read: "This church is the only church
authorised by God to represent the Lord Jesus
Christ." Is such a church part of the true Body of
Christ? If it is, then the attitude of its members
must cause our Lord considerable grief. It is tan-
tamount to crucifying him afresh. If only we who
profess the Name of Christ could see what we do
to our Lord when we choose to disobey his commands. If we did, then the Church would be very
different. How tragic that our Lord was wounded
at Calvary by his enemies but now he is being
wounded in the house of his friends.

For reading & meditation – Zechariah 13:1-9

OCTOBER 20

If it wasn't for you

"Who are you, Lord?" Saul asked. "I am Jesus, whom you are persecuting," he replied.
Acts 9:5

Do you believe our Lord is pained when, for example, we make no effort to be reconciled to those we have offended, when we put our denominational interests above Christian unity, or when we introduce our selfish ambitions into a kingdom that is based on self-giving? I believe he is in anguish when we do such things. "He was wounded *for* our transgressions," said the prophet Isaiah (53:5, KJV), but there is a sense in which he is wounded *by* our transgressions also. Thankfully he remains faithful to us even when we do not remain faithful to him.

For reading & meditation – Acts 9:1-19

OCTOBER 21

The true dynamic

But I, when I am lifted up from the earth, will draw all men to myself.
John 12:32

*W*e move on now to consider yet another vantage point from which we can contemplate the cross: the manner by which it captivates the attention of the men and women. This we might refer to as the magnetic cross. Some strange, powerful dynamic flows from the cross that draws more people than any other aspect of his ministry. As the centuries have proved, people can become interested in Christ for all manner of reasons – his pure personality, his moral teaching, his supreme example, and so on. But unless they are drawn to the Christ of the cross there can be no true salvation. It is the Christ of the cross who saves.

For reading & meditation – John 12:20-36

OCTOBER 22

Why the cross draws

*This is how God showed his love among us: He sent
his one and only Son into the world ...*
1 John 4:9

*P*ascal, the French philosopher, said: "If we could
see God as he really is then there would not be
such a thing as a sinner left in the world." Those
are powerful words. What drives us away from God
are our misconceptions of him. When we see him
as he really is – unbounding Love – then we are
not driven from him but drawn towards him. Love,
it has been said, is the greatest force in the world.
That being so, then Calvary is the greatest exhibi-
tion of that force. Its magnetism has touched my
heart. I hope it has touched yours too.

For reading & meditation – 1 John 4:7-21

OCTOBER 23

Heaven's strategy

Just as Moses lifted up the snake in the desert, so the Son of Man must be lifted up ...
John 3:14

Sin has blinded our eyes to the reality of God. We are not sure that he loves us enough to provide a way out of our sin and back to himself. The cross, however, lays that idea to rest. The uplifted Christ shows us that God loves us enough to give his own Son to die for us, and when we see God as he is – true unbounding Love – we are strangely drawn to him. Our Lord talked much about the love of God in his messages to the multitudes but they never comprehended that love fully until they saw it at Calvary. There he laid bare the heart of the Eternal and revealed the beauty and perfection of his love.

For reading & meditation – John 3:1-21

OCTOBER 24

We might become heirs

*... so that, having been justified by
his grace, we might become heirs ...*
Titus 3:7

*W*hen, many years ago, I looked at the cross and
saw what Christ did for me, a lost and hell-
deserving sinner, the sight of it drew my heart out
through my eyes in hot adoring tears of love.
Alexander Whyte, the great Scottish preacher,
stood in his pulpit one Sunday and announced:
"This past week I have discovered who is the most
wicked man in Edinburgh. And I am now going to
name him." As the congregation waited with bated
breath to see whom he would name he said very
quietly and with tears running down his face:
"Alexander Whyte."

For reading & meditation – Titus 3:1-11

OCTOBER 25

Beer into furniture

*... the gospel ... is the power of God for
the salvation of everyone who believes ...*
Romans 1:16

*T*he cross lifts us out of sin and lifts sin out of us.
A newly converted man who had previously been
known for his drunken and irresponsible behaviour
was speaking in an open-air service about Christ's
power to change. Suddenly his message was
interrupted by a heckler who shouted out: "You
don't really believe Christ turned water into wine
do you?" Quick as a flash he replied: "He has done
something better than that. He has turned beer
into furniture in my house. It takes power to
accomplish that – the power of the cross.

For reading & meditation – Romans 1:8-17

Come and die

If anyone would come after me,
he must ... take up his cross ...
Mark 8:34

*S*ummoning the crowds, our Lord told them bluntly that if they decided to be his followers then they must be willing to carry a cross. Obviously our Lord was not intending his followers to understand they would be literally crucified, but was using the word "cross" in a symbolic sense. So what did he mean? He meant that his followers should be prepared to have a deathblow delivered to their natural self-interest and to live for God's interests. And this was not intended to be one dramatic gesture of self-abnegation but a continuous one.

For reading & meditation – Mark 8:31-38

OCTOBER 27

Outside the camp

*Let us, then, go to him outside the
camp, bearing the disgrace he bore.*
Hebrews 13:13

*T*aking up the cross means far more than putting
up with irritations and frustrations. The cross we
are to take up on Christ's behalf is a chosen
cross. It is something, if we so desire, we can avoid.
It has to do, I believe, with living so closely to
Christ, identifying so completely with him, that
the disgrace he suffered falls on us. Get this fact
firmly fixed in your mind – there is a disgrace
associated with the gospel. There is a shame at
the heart of the cross and it must be borne. The
issue then is this: those who follow Christ and com-
mit themselves to him wholeheartedly can expect
to suffer the same obloquy and shame.

For reading & meditation – Hebrews 13:7-21

OCTOBER 28

Not our shame – his

In fact, everyone who wants to live a godly life in Christ Jesus will be persecuted ...
2 Timothy 3:12

*T*here is a choice to be made, and if you are willing to be definite in discipleship – and by that I mean committed to taking up your cross – then you must be prepared for the fact that it may involve a degree of suffering and shame. Many reading these lines will know what it means to be the butt of a joke or the object of ridicule because they "stand up for Jesus" in their social circle, school or place of work. You are made to feel you are not part of the set – "outside the camp". But don't fret about this – bear it willingly.

For reading & meditation – 2 Timothy 3:10-17

OCTOBER 29

Play His Part

*And anyone who does not carry his cross
and follow me cannot be my disciple.*
Luke 14:27

*I*an Macpherson tells a delightful story of a couple
who went to see the famous Passion Play in
Oberammergau, in which the story of Christ and
his crucifixion is acted out. The husband thought
it would be a good idea to have his wife photo-
graph him bearing it. He found it was too heavy
for him. "It's heavier than I thought," he remarked
and, turning to the actor, said: "Why is it so
heavy?" The actor replied: "Sir, if I did not feel
the full weight of his cross I could not play his
part." We must all feel the weight of the cross if
we are to play his part.

For reading & meditation – Luke 14:25-35

OCTOBER 30

Another shoulder

For my yoke is easy and my burden is light.
Matthew 11:30

Christians who bear Christ's cross, find to their delight that there is another shoulder beneath it in addition to their own. One preacher, B.D. Johns, put it like this: "He who has been on the cross for us has promised to be under the cross with us." So the next time you undertake some uncongenial task for the sake of Christ, need to subordinate your own interests, suffer some mild or not so mild ostracism, experience setbacks in your vocation or profession, or become the subject of covert sneers, then take heart – under the cross is not only your shoulder but the shoulder of the Crucified One. And Christ helps lift us as well as the cross by his sustaining power.

For reading & meditation – Matthew 11:25-30

OCTOBER 31

NOVEMBER

A man came among us

You ... are controlled ... by the Spirit, if
the Spirit of God lives in you.
Romans 8:9

John Wesley was a preacher and a missionary as a young man, yet did not have a personal relationship with Christ. John Wesley had a surprise when he went to a meeting, to hear someone reading Martin Luther's preface to the book of Romans. John Wesley felt his own heart "strangely warmed". This unexpected warming of the heart sent a moral cleansing through the soul of Britain and the world. Cornwall, in England was greatly affected by the ministry of John Wesley. A visitor remarked: "You seem to be a very temperate people here." A miner replied: "There came a man among us once, and his name was John Wesley."

For reading & meditation – Romans 8:1-17

NOVEMBER 1

The ordinariness of Jesus

Jesus answered: "Don't you know me, Philip, even after I have been among you such a long time?"
John 14:9

*P*hilip, in the passage before us today, seemed to miss the fact that the One standing before him was God. Was it because Jesus looked so ordinary? Philip asked Christ where God could be seen! Human nature is always more attracted to the spectacular than the truly great. If God had come to earth in a chariot of fire, multitudes would have knelt before him. But he so blended the sublime with the normal that only the few saw the sublime was there. If he had moved among people with a shining face and dazzling apparel aristocrats would have sought him out.

For reading & meditation – John 14:1-14

NOVEMBER 2

In for a surprise

*Therefore keep watch, because you do not
know on what day your Lord will come.*
Matthew 24:42

*T*here seems to be a good deal of misunderstanding about the second coming of Christ in certain Christian circles. A young graduate's tutor said: 'Jesus somehow got the idea he was going to come back one day, but that idea did not come from God. Some of his ideas were from God, but some were not. I slipped into a church in the USA some years ago and heard a preacher admit: "I do not believe that Christ will ever return to this earth." I thought to myself: "My friend, you are in for a great surprise."

For reading & meditation – Matthew 24:36-51

NOVEMBER 3

The guided life

... but no-one laid a hand on him,
because his time had not yet come.
John 7:30

*E*arly in his ministry Christ was aware that he was moving towards a powerful and pivotal hour. The passage before us today shows how the Jews sought to arrest him in the Temple. But they were unable to effect their evil purpose because, as the Evangelist explains: "his time had not yet come." It is important to observe that our Lord never took the matter of divine protection for granted. He got his instructions from his Father, through waiting upon him in prayer. Perhaps if we spent more time in prayer we might have fewer reasons to rue the calamities that seem to befall us.

For reading & meditation – John 7:25-44

NOVEMBER 4

When God laughs

The One enthroned in heaven laughs;
the Lord scoffs at them.
Psalm 2:4

*A*s we read Biblical history we see times when it looked as if events were out of control and then, suddenly, a particular occurrence turned the whole situation around. When God's time arrives, he intervenes, and the situation is seen as contributing to his purpose, not anyone else's. God can arise and confound his enemies at any moment: "The One enthroned in heaven laughs". He sees the little people of this earth strutting so arrogantly through their days. He knows that at a word he can destroy them all. He could do it, but he won't, for divine purposes are being worked out.

For reading & meditation – Psalm 2:1-12

NOVEMBER 5

~~//~~

"What's in it for me?"

Set you minds on things above, not on earthly things.
Colossians 3:2

I don't know about you, but I find it deeply moving that our Lord's one desire was this – that he might glorify the Father. How different are our attitudes when called upon to face a crisis. I think it is because we are being brainwashed by a world that is filled with self-interest and self-concern. If we can't change the questions people ask when they come into the church we ought to be able to change the questions they ask once they are there. Is this where the Church is failing? Brainwashed Christians need another kind of washing – washing by the water of the Word (Eph. 5:26).

For reading & meditation – Colossians 3:1-17

NOVEMBER 6

Saved in eternity!

And he made known to us the mystery of his will ... which he purposed in Christ ...
Ephesians 1:9

"*F*or you granted him authority over all people that he might give eternal life to all those you have given him" (John 17:2). These words imply that at some point in the past Christ, the second Person of the Trinity, was placed in a position of authority and assigned the task of giving eternal life to as many as God foreordained. Our salvation is a planned salvation. It is not an afterthought, but was conceived in the mind of the Trinity long before time began. Can you see what this means? Our salvation is safe! "God thought it, Christ bought it, the Spirit wrought it, and though the devil fought it – thank God I've got it."

For reading & meditation – Ephesians 1:1-14

NOVEMBER 7

~☿~

Jubilant praise

*He came and took the scroll from the right
hand of him who sat on the throne.*
Revelation 5:7

*T*he matter of dealing with sin should be handed
over specifically to the Son. With the agreement
of the other two members of the Trinity he was
made responsible not only for the inanimate
creation but the world of men and women also.
John is perplexed that no one is great enough or
strong enough to open the books of history. Then
suddenly the Lion of the tribe of Judah steps
forward and all heaven breaks out in jubilant
praise. And why? Because Jesus Christ is the Lord
of history. Indeed, as it is often said – history is
His-story.

For reading & meditation – Revelation 5:1-14

NOVEMBER 8

Marked out in eternity

All that the Father gives me will come to me ...
John 6:37

*G*od the Father gave to Christ a special group of people who are destined to enjoy the blessings of salvation and live with him forever. God chose them and God is the One who *draws* them. It is as if the Father said to the Son: "I am giving you a special group of people and I want you to save them for me." Our salvation was forethought, foreseen, and foreordained. What a thought with which to begin the day! Let the wonder of it wrap itself around your soul. You are a planned inheritor of the kingdom – a kingdom foreseen before the foundation of the world.

For reading & meditation – John 6:25-40

NOVEMBER 9

Homesick for Heaven?

I am the Lord ... I will not give my glory to another ...
Isaiah 42:8

I often wonder to myself how much of the former glory Christ was able to remember when he was here on earth. Did celestial sounds drift from time to time into his consciousness, or were they there all the while? We do not know. We do know that our Lord voluntarily surrendered for the period of thirty-three years the right to be worshipped, the right to the glory that belonged to God. Do we sense here in the Saviour a homesickness for heaven? Perhaps so. I'm glad, though, that his desire to return to heaven was not as great as his determination to complete the work his Father had given him to do.

For reading & meditation – Isaiah 42:1-13

NOVEMBER 10

No attitude problem

*Your attitude should be the
same as that of Christ Jesus ...*
Philippians 2:5

*W*hen John baptised him in the River Jordan,
the heavens opened, a dove descended, and God
declared: "This is my Son, whom I love; with him
I am well pleased" (Matt. 3:17). Christ had not
done anything yet but obviously for thirty years he
had delighted the Father's heart. Jesus was great
by what he did, but he was great also by the
attitude with which he did it. Throughout his life
he had a heart that was ready to obey, an ear that
was ready to hear, and a will that was ready to be
subject to the Father. He put his finger on the essence of that which glorifies God – self-giving love.

For reading & meditation – Philippians 2:1-11

NOVEMBER   11

A day for decision

*"Who do you say I am?" Simon Peter answered,
"You are the Christ, the Son of the living God."*
Matthew 16:15-16

*T*here is another very important aspect of being
a follower of Christ – *we must be clear as to who
Jesus is*. I would go as far as to say that anyone
who is not convinced that Jesus is the Son of God
cannot be a Christian. We fool ourselves when we
look at people who live good moral lives and on
that basis alone, describe them as Christians. Good,
upright, moral living is required of every Christian, but that is not the first mark of being one of
Christ's disciples. The first mark is to be convinced
about the Person of Christ – who he is and why he
came. True Christians believe that the Word was
made flesh and dwelt among us.

For reading & meditation – Matthew 16:13-20

NOVEMBER   12

A long prayer session

... he always lives to intercede for them.
Hebrews 7:25

*J*ust think of it – at this very moment our Lord sits on the throne interceding for you and me. And he has been engaged in this task of praying for his people since he arrived on the throne close on 2000 years ago. This makes it the longest prayer session in history! As the disciples overheard the words of Jesus "I pray for them" (John 17:9) how it must have brought comfort and consolation to their hearts. And as he continued, "I am not praying for the world, but for those you have given me, for they are yours," they would have gained even more comfort as they sensed that he was praying not for the world in general but for them in particular.

For reading & meditation – Hebrews 7:18-28

NOVEMBER 13

A little means a lot

You did not choose me, but I chose you
and appointed you to go and bear fruit ...
John 15:16

*J*esus said: "And glory has come to me through them." The disciples often quarrelled with one another yet here our Lord is saying quite categorically: "... glory has come to me through *them*." An observer watching the disciples over a period of time might have concluded that they were quarrelsome, jealous, dull and blundering, and seen nothing more. But Jesus saw that they were definitely committed to him, and had already brought him glory by their obedient trust. Their commitment was perhaps little, but to Jesus the little meant a lot.

For reading & meditation – John 15:1-16

NOVEMBER 14

Who cares?

If ... God clothes the grass of the field ...
will he not much more clothe you ...?
Matthew 6:30

"*I* will remain in the world no longer, but they are still in the world, and I am coming to you. Holy Father, protect them by the power of your name – the name you gave me – so that they may be one as we are one" (John 17:11). The focus of Christ's petition is found in the two words "protect them". His heart's greatest desire – that they might be divinely kept and divinely protected. Oh, if only we could get hold of this fact – that our Lord's concern for us is greater than the concern we have for ourselves. The awareness of it, rather than the theory, would make a tremendous impact on our souls.

For reading & meditation – Matthew 6:25-34

NOVEMBER 15

The knowledge of God

I will declare your name to my brothers ...
Hebrews 2:12

*N*ames in the Bible are more than designations, they are definitions. In the Old Testament period, when God entered into a new relationship with his people or disclosed another aspect of his character, he revealed a new Name. The more we know his Name the more we know of him. But God's revelation through his Names was limited, that is, until Jesus came. Christ revealed through his life and works the nature of God in a way that no name could possibly do. It is that knowledge – the knowledge of God which only Jesus could truly unfold that our Saviour is referring to here.

For reading & meditation – Hebrews 2:10-18

One Name, one way

Jacob said, "Please tell me your name."
Genesis 32:29

*T*he Father, as the Scripture makes clear in so many different places, sent the Son into the world to declare his Name, to unfold his character, to reveal his essential nature. The revelation brought by the Son has done more to explain the mystery of who God is than anyone or anything else. There is no true and real knowledge of God except in and through the Person of his Son, Jesus Christ. Those who try to come to God some other way are described in John 10:1 as "thieves and robbers". To bypass Christ in an effort to get to God is to rob Christ of his glory. Heaven will never stand for that!

For reading & meditation – Genesis 32:22-32

NOVEMBER 17

Jesus is God

I and the Father are one.
John 10:30

" ... So that they may be one as we are one."
Christ is praying here that the same unity which
exists between himself and his Father might be
known also among his disciples. Jehovah's Wit-
nesses do not believe Jesus is God. Their
understanding of the above is that Jesus did not
mean one in essence; he meant one in purpose. But
what a staggering thought it is that the carpenter
of Nazareth is one with the Father – God in human
form. I remember being struck by this thought on
the very first day of my conversion. I could not get
over it then, and I have not been able to get over it
since. Be staggered by it if you will, but never let
go of it. Jesus Christ is God.

For reading & meditation – John 10:22-42

NOVEMBER 18

The Big Picture

... may have power ... to grasp how wide and long
and high and deep is the love of Christ ...
Ephesians 3:18

Jesus' entrance into the world by way of the virgin birth was the first step in the carrying out of a plan. He came because God had handed to him the people whom he had foreordained in eternity, and said, in effect: "They are not fit for heaven as they are; they would not enjoy me nor I them, so I give them to you, to save and to sanctify. Make them a people in whom I can have the greatest pleasure." See the Big Picture. There's much more to salvation than just having our sins forgiven – wonderful though that may be. Jesus died not just to make us fit for heaven but fit to enjoy heaven.

For reading & meditation – Ephesians 3:1-21

NOVEMBER 19

~ ※ ~

Forsaken by all

Then all the disciples deserted him and fled.
Matthew 26:56

*W*e have no way of knowing with certainty what would have occupied the disciples' thoughts in those dark days between the cross and the resurrection, but it is clear from what we read that they were caught up in a deep spiritual crisis. Would Jesus have revised his prayer if he had prayed it following the act of desertion by his disciples? I believe Christ knew his disciples would forsake him, but he knew also that despite their fears, their hesitancies, their denials and their doubts, deep down in their hearts they would be undergirded by the conviction that what he said would come to pass.

For reading & meditation – Matthew 26:47-56

NOVEMBER 20

New life for everyone!

He is not here; he has risen, just as he said. Come and see the place where he lay. Then go quickly and tell his disciples: 'He has risen from the dead and is going ahead of you into Galilee. There you will see him.' Now I have told you.
Matthew 28:6, 7

*T*he incarnation, temptation, agony, crucifixion, and resurrection were all part of God's plan to make us fit for heaven and fit to enjoy heaven. But what we must remember is this – the incarnation, temptation, agony and crucifixion would have been as nothing unless our Lord had broken through the grave and came back from death. The empty tomb is the proof that God's plan had worked.

For reading & meditation – Matthew 28:1-15

NOVEMBER 21

We are kept

... but now you have returned to the Shepherd and Overseer of your souls.
1 Peter 2:25

*B*ut just how did the Master keep and protect his disciples while he was with them? One way was by his personal petitions on their behalf. On one occasion he said to Simon Peter: "Satan has asked to sift you ... but I have prayed for you" (Luke 22:31-32). Another way was by his frequent warnings and cautions. People were bringing little children to Jesus to have him touch them, but the disciples rebuked them. When Jesus saw this, he was indignant. He said to them, "Let the little children come to me, and do not hinder them ..." (Mark 10:13-14). He kept them also by his teaching.

For reading & meditation – 1 Peter 2:15-25

NOVEMBER 22

A son of hell

*... Jesus replied, "Have I not chosen you,
the Twelve? Yet one of you is a devil!"*
John 6:70

Jesus is referring to Judas, the one who would
betray him. The treachery of Judas was prophesied
in Psalms 41 and 109, and our Lord is saying in
effect, "The prophets saw this coming centuries
ago, and Judas, 'the son of hell', is going to fulfil
their predictions to the letter." We will never be
able to fully explain why Jesus allowed Judas to
be part of the disciples' band, but we know enough
of Jesus to be able to trust him when we can't understand him. That is what we must do with all
unanswerable questions – trust him.

For reading & meditation – John 6:68-71

NOVEMBER 23

Judas the thief

*He did not say this because he cared about
the poor but because he was a thief ...*
John 12:6

*J*udas walked with the Lord day by day, sat and
listened to him teach, heard the most amazing truth
fall from his lips, but he never comprehended it
or took it in. He was also, as our text for today
shows, a man of base character – a thief. His
dishonest act was not something done on the spur
of the moment; it was premeditated and contrived.
Finally, it was *predicted* of Judas that he would be
lost. The Old Testament Scriptures point clearly
to this fact. Judas was already destined for hell. In
a sense Judas was always lost, for he had never
truly been saved.

For reading & meditation – John 12:1-11

NOVEMBER 24

True dedication

I have come to do your will, O God.
Hebrews 10:7

*S*o what Our Lord is saying at this point is that all he has, and is, he is now giving entirely and utterly to God so that his disciples may in turn be truly sanctified. If we were to paraphrase his words they would read something like this: "For their sake I dedicate the whole of my being to you." The Son of God has devoted himself utterly to our redemption, and has given himself to it with unswerving devotion. Everything else is excluded so that this one thing can be achieved. Has there ever been a dedication more wonderful than that?

For reading & meditation – Hebrews 10:1-18

Saved to serve!

Therefore go and make disciples of all nations ...
Matthew 28:19

*W*hen Christ had returned to heaven, the angels inquired of him: "Master, what plans do you have for ensuring that your gospel will be preached throughout the world?" The Lord explained that he had left the task in the hands of his followers. The angels seemed surprised at this, and said: "But Master, your disciples are so fickle and unreliable, what if they fail? What other arrangements have you made?" Solemnly the Lord looked at them and said: "None, this is the only way my gospel can be made known. I have no other plan!"

For reading & meditation – Matthew 28:16-20

NOVEMBER 26

We know!

*... the Father himself loves you
because you have loved me ...*
John 16:27

"*T*hey (meaning the elect) know that you have sent me." These words must not be taken to mean that Christ has no love or concern for those who will not come to him. He still provides them with the benefits of what theologians call "common grace" – the blessings of life, such as air to breathe, food to eat, and so on. God loves all his creation, but the fact has to be faced, he has a special love for those who come to know him through Christ. We who are his children must glory in it. We can be sure we are Christ's when we are able to look into the face of the Father and say: "We know that you have sent him into the world." We know.

For reading & meditation – John 16:25-33

NOVEMBER   27

The hope of glory

*... the glorious riches of this mystery,
which is Christ in you, the hope of glory.*
Colossians 1:27

*W*hichever member of the Trinity you come across in Scripture, you never get a sense that he is performing merely from a sense of duty. What they do they do with delight. At this point our Lord is just about to go to the cross and to die one of the most fiendishly cruel deaths ever devised by man yet his thought is not of himself but of continuing in the task which God had given him – to reveal and continue to reveal the Father's heart to the world. To be "in Christ" is wonderful, but for Christ to be in me is equally wonderful. Perhaps even more so.

For reading & meditation – Colossians 1:15-29

NOVEMBER   28

"Speech without a stutter"

*In the past God spoke ... through the prophets at
many times and in various ways ...*
Hebrews 1:1

*G*od has spoken to all humankind through Jesus
Christ in a manner far greater and clearer than
when he spoke through the prophets. When you
read the Old Testament you are hearing the
message of God, but a message that is incomplete.
In the New Testament, however – especially the
Gospels – you find a new voice that gathers up
the syllables and phrases in which God spoke in
the Old Testament and merges them into one
complete and final discourse. God's Word and
message to humanity has been fully uttered in and
through his Son. "In him," as one great theologian
put it, "God speaks without a stutter."

For reading & meditation – Hebrews 1:1

NOVEMBER 29

"Go to hell then"

*... in these last days he has spoken to us by his Son,
whom he appointed heir of all things ...*
Hebrews 1:2

A rather belligerent doctor once said to a missionary: "I don't believe in Christ or God." The missionary said gently: "Go to hell then." That is where rejection of God and Christ leads. Christ is the heir of all things because all things were made for him and by him. The touch of Christ is on all creation; everything is made in its inner structure to work in his way. When it works in his way, it works well, but when it works some other way it works to its own destination. Live according to Christ and you live; live against him and you perish – eternally.

For reading & meditation – Hebrews 1:1-2

NOVEMBER 30

DECEMBER

The stamp of God's image

The Son is ... the exact representation of his being,
sustaining all things by his powerful word.
Hebrews 1:3

*M*en and women look to nature in the attempt to
see the image of God. They view the sunrises and
sunsets, the rivers and the oceans, and wonder if
God is like that. But the storm rages, thunder rolls,
lightning strikes, earthquakes demolish whole
townships, and their concept of God is shaken. To
know God as he really is we must look into the
face of Jesus – the stamp of God's very image.
The question that then arises is not so much is Jesus
like God, but is God like Jesus? And because he
is, then despite any appearances to the contrary,
we must affirm him as good.

For reading & meditation – Hebrews 1:1-3

DECEMBER 1

"Staggering to a throne"

*After he had provided purification for sins, he sat
down at the right hand of the Majesty in heaven.*
Hebrews 1:3

The central purpose of Christ's coming to this
earth was not to be an example or a teacher, but to
be a Saviour and a Redeemer. "You are to give
him the name Jesus, because he will save his
people from their sins," was the divine prediction
(Matt. 1:21). "From their sins" implies he frees us
from the power that sin has over us. Is it any wonder that the early Christians, when looking for a
declaration that would sum up the Christian faith,
settled on the words "Jesus is Lord?" They saw
that he is Lord not only by appointment but also
by accomplishment.

For reading & meditation – Hebrews 1:1-3

DECEMBER 2

Higher than angels!

*So he became as much superior to the angels as the
name he has inherited is superior to theirs.*
Hebrews 1:4

*W*hen God brought his Son into the world, he
commanded that all the angels worship him. The
worship of angels at Bethlehem is yet another clear
testimony to the deity of our Lord. He is seen to
be greater than angels by the demonstration of their
worship. But what are angels? They are the servants and ministers of God – depicted in this passage as wind and fire. They are not as prominent
today as they were in Bible days because the Holy
Spirit is now resident in the world to lead and
guide. But make no mistake about it – they are
still around and at work. One of them might even
be on a mission to help you this very day.

For reading & meditation – Hebrews 1:4-9

DECEMBER 3

On and on, for ever

*But you remain the same, and
your years will never end.*
Hebrews 1:12

*W*ickedness and wrongdoing have the stamp of
death upon them, for right (or righteousness) is on
the throne. God's day is coming. Verse 10   reminds
us that Christ sits upon the throne as both the
Originator and Sustainer of the universe, and shares
the eternity of God. Created things will perish, but
that which is eternal will remain. Scientists often
talk about "the second law of thermodynamics" –
the degenerative faculty in the universe. This is
what the writer of Hebrews is talking about. All
created things will grow old like a garment, but the
One who made them will not.

For reading & meditation – Hebrews 1:8-12

DECEMBER   4

Tongues that are stilled

*Are not all angels ministering spirits
sent to serve those who will inherit salvation?*
Hebrews 1:14

*T*he superiority of Christ over angels puts the matter once again in the form of an interrogation: "To which of the angels did God ever say, 'Sit at my right hand ...'?" (v. 13). Here the Son is seen as eternally enthroned and waiting in that position for the ultimate subjugation of all who oppose his rule. In the closing words of the first chapter we are therefore brought back to the thought with which we began – everything will conclude at his feet. "What are angels?" the writer of the book of Hebrews is asking. Servants. But the Son? The Son – ah – he is God.

For reading & meditation – Hebrews 1:13-14

DECEMBER 5

Pay attention!

*... how shall we escape if
we ignore such a great salvation?*
Hebrews 2:3

*H*ow sad that so many Christians seem willing to give their attention to anything but the Word of God. What can be more heartbreaking to a pastor than to preach the truths of God's Word to people week after week – truths that can set them free and transform their whole existence – and to see them miss God's best by their failure to pay attention? This is why Jesus had to say again and again: "He who has ears, let him hear." If we don't pay attention to what Christ says then we will, by default, have to pay attention to the difficulties that life presents. We either heed the helm or we heed the rocks.

For reading & meditation – Hebrews 2:1-4

D E C E M B E R   6

Dignity vs depravity

But we see Jesus, who was made a little lower than the angels, now crowned with glory and honour ...
Hebrews 2:9

*A*dam and Eve sinned and as a result the whole human race now finds itself in futility. The statement "Yet at present we do not see everything subject to him" focuses attention on the state of the human race from Adam's day to this – we struggle to have dominion over the earth but the depravity in our hearts prevents us from fully exercising it. The writer turns our eyes to One who has come among us: He was "made for a little while lower than the angels", lived in perfect obedience, overcame death, and has won the right to lift us to even greater heights than Adam and Eve would have reached had they not sinned.

For reading & meditation – Hebrews 2:5-9

DECEMBER 7

All one family

So Jesus is not ashamed to call them brothers.
Hebrews 2:11b

*I*magine Jesus went into the wilderness to be tempted on Monday, preached the Sermon on the Mount on Tuesday, worked the Miracle of the Feeding of the Five Thousand on Wednesday, gave the Olivet Discourse on Thursday, died on the cross on Friday – would he have been able in that time to enter into *all* our sufferings? Of course not. Because he *fully* entered into our fears and pressures, he is now fully one with us. He is truly part of the human family and we, by his redemption, are truly part of his.

For reading & meditation – Hebrews 2:10-13

Satan's lost whip

*... that by his death he might destroy
him who holds the power of death ...*
Hebrews 2:14

*T*hroughout the ages, the biggest single whip that
Satan has used to strike terror into hearts is the
fear of death. Our Lord tasted death for us, and by
so doing has taken the whip out of the devil's hands.
The devil is still active in many ways, but through
Christ's victory on Calvary he has lost the power
to whip into subjection those who are his. The fear
of death stops many entering into the joys of life.
But not a true Christian. When Jesus went down
into death, it was death that died, not he. In him
we live – and how!

For reading & meditation – Hebrews 2:14-15

DECEMBER 9

The sympathising Saviour

*Because he himself suffered when he was tempted,
he is able to help those who are being tempted.*
Hebrews 2:18

*H*amlet speaks of the "heartaches and the thousand natural shocks that flesh is heir to". Does he exaggerate? Hardly. When we think of the complex spiritual ills of our race, the hurts, disappointments, rejection, cruelty, woundedness, and so on, we wonder how can Christ meet them all. But because he has felt the whole gamut of human suffering, he can. When beset by temptation, sit in the presence of Jesus and let his power and your faith meet. Then, just as when the woman touched the hem of his garment, the ancient miracle will be worked once more. You will touch him and be whole again.

For reading & meditation – Hebrews 2:16-18

DECEMBER 10

Greater than Moses

*Jesus has been found worthy of
greater honour than Moses ...*
Hebrews 3:3

*G*od had spoken powerfully to his ancient people
through Moses, and it was the conviction that he
was the mouthpiece of God which had helped to
hold the nation together down the running
centuries. The main aim of the writer in this
passage is to concentrate our attention on the
concept of God's house, in which both Moses and
Jesus served faithfully, but in a very different ca-
pacity. The word "house" refers not to a building
but to a community of people – the people of God.
And all of God's people, both in Old Testament
times and New Testament times, are considered
part of his "house".

For reading & meditation – Hebrews 3:1-6

DECEMBER 11

The cure is Christ

Everything is uncovered and laid bare before the
eyes of him to whom we must give account.
Hebrews 4:13

*T*he Word of God, we are told, is not merely a document, but is living and active. The words are alive because the Word is alive – the Word that is bigger than men's words. Often when I have been counselling someone I have heard them say: "It feels as if a knot has been untied deep inside me." Ever since I became a minister of the gospel, I have struggled to find the genesis of human problems. What causes all the complexes and complications that arise in the human personality? I still don't know all the causes, but I certainly know the cure. It is Christ – the living Word.

For reading & meditation – Hebrews 4:11-13

DECEMBER 12

The throne of grace

Let us then approach the throne
of grace with confidence ...
Hebrews 4:16

*T*he wonderful thing about Christ, the Great High
Priest, the writer of Hebrews continues, is that
because he has been in our condition, he is able to
sympathize with our every circumstance – sin
excepted. He has felt every pressure we feel,
every allurement we face, every pull we encounter, every temptation we are called upon to endure
– and never once did he yield to them. Because of
this, we can draw nigh to the throne of grace with
the confidence that we are going to find One there
who is fully sensitive to our problems and our
needs.

For reading & meditation – Hebrews 4:14-16

DECEMBER 13

Greatest

You are a priest for ever, in the order of Melchizedek.
Hebrews 5:6

*O*ne of the most subtle arguments used by Satan is this: "The Son of God had an advantage over you. He had no sinful nature. You haven't the strength to withstand. God will forgive you. After all – that's his job." Though Jesus was God he humbled himself to become man. On the cross he came to grips with the problem of human sin. He experienced every temptation that comes our way. And finally, the writer points out he was appointed by God, just as Aaron was, yet with this difference: God did not say to Christ, "You are my servant," but "You are my Son."

For reading & meditation – Hebrews 5:1-6

DECEMBER 14

A sense of sin

... he was heard because of his reverent submission.
Hebrews 5:7

*Y*ears ago I used to puzzle over the fact that our Lord seemed to demonstrate more apprehension and personal struggle in the garden than he did when being nailed to the cross. He experienced what we often describe as "a sense of sin." He had suffered before, but never like this. Every cell in his being cried out to be delivered, yet neverthe-less his obedience remained intact. Jesus' time of agony illustrates the fact that when we throw on God's side all our willingness, he throws on our side all his power. Hardly any thought can be greater than that.

For reading & meditation – Hebrews 5:7-10

DECEMBER 15

The anchoria

We have this hope as an anchor
for the soul, firm and secure.
Hebrews 6:19

*T*he hope that one day we will enter into the presence of God and experience all the joys of heaven is, says the writer to the Hebrews, like an anchor for the soul – firm and secure. Christ is our "Forerunner" and has fastened "the rope of hope" to the divine *anchoria* – the throne of God. In ancient times no one ever followed the high priest into the Most Holy Place, but this new High Priest – Jesus – guarantees to every believer the promise of confident access into the very presence of the living God. Jesus our Forerunner is there; we can follow also.

For reading & meditation – Hebrews 6:19-20

DECEMBER 16

Just what we need

*He sacrificed for their sins once
for all when he offered himself.*
Hebrews 7:27

"**S**uch a high priest meets our need – one who
is holy, blameless, pure, set apart from sinners,
exalted above the heavens" (v26). I am sure you
have noticed that the writer to the Hebrews
simply cannot take his eyes off Christ. He is
writing to buffeted, confused and persecuted
Christians who are being tempted to return to the
pageantry of the past, but over and over again he
repeats his one theme – Jesus is just what we need.
Our Lord does not need to offer sacrifices every
day. He has offered himself and this one offering
suffices for time and eternity.

For reading & meditation – Hebrews 7:26-28

DECEMBER 17

The original design

*They serve at a sanctuary that is a
copy and shadow of what is in heaven.*
Hebrews 8:5

*T*he writer to the Hebrews tells us that Jesus is
not standing before the throne, but is seated there.
His sacrificial work is done and the effects of his
great sacrifice go on for ever. Our Lord by his
sacrifice on the cross opened up a way into the
very presence of God – the Holy of Holies –
whereby soiled sinners could pass through the open
court, right past the ranks of worshipping angels,
and stand before the very throne of God himself
just as if we had never sinned. Can anything in
heaven or earth be more wonderful?

For reading & meditation – Hebrews 8:1-5

DECEMBER 18

The new covenant

*For if there had been nothing wrong
with that first covenant, no place
would have been sought for another.*
Hebrews 8:7

Jesus, our Great High Priest, mediates a more excellent covenant than the former since it is founded on better promises. A covenant between God and man must never be thought of as a contract between two equal parties. God is always the sole initiator, and having laid down the terms of the covenant, invites men and women to join with him in it. God promised through Jeremiah that the day would dawn when a new covenant would be given that would be infinitely more effective than the old. Thanks be to God – that day has arrived.

For reading & meditation – Hebrews 8:6-9

DECEMBER 19

Inside out!

*This is the covenant I will make with
the house of Israel after that time ...*
Hebrews 8:10

"*T*his cup is the new covenant in my blood"
(1 Cor. 11:25). This is a new covenant made not
between God and us but between God and his Son,
the Lord Jesus Christ. When we receive Christ then
because we are in him everything specified in the
covenant is available to us. Just as we hunger to
belong to someone in the natural world, so we hunger
also in the spiritual realm. Through Christ we
belong to God – our spiritual identity crisis is over
and our restless hearts find their home in him.

For reading & meditation – Hebrews 8:10-13

DECEMBER 20

Key to effective worship

*... the way into the Most Holy Place had
not yet been disclosed as long as the first
tabernacle was still standing.*
Hebrews 9:8

*O*ne of the most important keys to effective
worship is a clear conscience. Don't you find it
difficult if not impossible to worship when you
have a guilty conscience? Worshippers in Old
Testament times did not have their consciences
cleansed, and therefore they had no rest. Thus they
had to return again and again to perform re-
peatedly the same rituals in an endless search for
peace. How privileged we are to have our consciences made clean by the blood of Christ. It
makes a world of difference to our worship.

For reading & meditation – Hebrews 9:1-10

DECEMBER 21

Christ's blood

How much more, then, will the blood of Christ ... cleanse our consciences ...
Hebrews 9:14

*D*oing things for God, and being active for him, cannot in itself quieten or subdue the guilty conscience. The new arrangement by which Christians are now to live, depends not on the work and activity of the worshipper but on the activity of Christ on our behalf. The ministry of Jesus, our Great High Priest, moves through the barrier of flesh into what we might describe as the Holy of Holies – our spirit, the inner man. Here, where the conscience resides, the value of Christ's blood is applied. It is not our activity that brings us peace but his activity on our behalf.

For reading & meditation – Hebrews 9:11-14

DECEMBER 22

No other way

... he has died as a ransom to set them free ...
Hebrews 9:15

*T*here is a reason why blood drips from almost every page of the Bible and it is this – without the shedding of blood there is no forgiveness. This may be repulsive but the point is – so is our sin. The penalty for sin is death, and the remedy for that is the death of Another. It was our blood that needed to be shed, but so great was Christ's love for us that he allowed his own blood to be shed – on our behalf. Let those who criticise the gospel try to come up with some answer. There isn't one. It took the death of the Son of God to bring us salvation. How dare we criticise it?

For reading & meditation – Hebrews 9:15-22

The three appearings

But now he has appeared ... to do away
with sin by the sacrifice of himself.
Hebrews 9:26

*I*t seems somewhat strange that the writer should say that heavenly things had to be purified by blood. Maybe, as one commentator puts it: "The heavens have a certain defilement through contact with the sins that are absolved in them." What a picture this is of the ministry of our Lord, who appeared in this world to take on the task of being our Great High Priest, and who now appears in the presence of God for us. Finally he will appear to the world once again, not this time in humility, but in garments of majesty and glory.

For reading & meditation – Hebrews 9:23-28

DECEMBER 24

One unchanging message

... it is impossible for the blood of
bulls and goats to take away sins.
Hebrews 10:4

*N*o worshipper was ever brought to what someone has described as "a real and enduring fellowship with God", for none ever lost the feelings of
guilt that sin inevitably brings. To the writer of
Hebrews, the very fact that the sin offerings were
made continually, year after year, was proof that
the old institutions, although divinely appointed,
were not the final answer. Yet how many pin their
hopes for salvation, even today, on shadows,
instead of taking hold of the reality which is Christ.
They prefer rituals instead of the Saviour. How
sad. How so very sad.

For reading & meditation – Hebrews 10:1-4

DECEMBER 25

What God is looking for

... I have come to do your will, O God.
Hebrews 10:7

"*S*acrifice and offering you did not desire, but a *body* you prepared for me" (v. 5). And the will of our Lord, functioning in a human body, never once acted independently. Throughout every moment of his life on earth he maintained a complete and utter dependence on the Father who indwelt him. That is the principle that God had longed to see in the universe – the principle of trust and confidence in the Father's purposes. What he looks for is what he saw perfectly in Jesus – a human will in a human frame demonstrating absolute trust in him.

For reading & meditation – Hebrews 10:5-10

DECEMBER 26

I can't remember that!

And where these have been forgiven,
there is no longer any sacrifice for sin.
Hebrews 10:18

*T*he Holy Spirit who, speaking through Jeremiah, promised all believers: "I will put my laws in their hearts ... write them on their minds." Just think of it – through the perfect sacrifice, our sins and lawless deeds are remembered no more. Sometimes you may be tempted to bring up those old reprehensible acts which have been forgiven and say to the Lord: "Don't you remember what I did and those awful things I was guilty of?" He simply shakes his head, looks at you with a smile, and says: "No, I'm sorry, I can't remember that."

For reading & meditation – Hebrews 10:11-18

DECEMBER 27

The unchanging Christ

Jesus Christ is the same yesterday
and today and for ever.
Hebrews 13:8

*A*lvin Toffler, in his book *Future Shock*, argues
that the quicker things happen, and the faster life
gets, the more stress is produced in the personality because we do not have time to adjust to the
necessary change. Life, if it is to be lived successfully, needs a centre of permanence, something to
which we can fasten our hope knowing it will never
shift. Jesus Christ is that centre of permanence.
What he is and was he ever will be. This changeless Christ is the great refuge of the Christian in a
world that is caught up in constant change.

For reading & meditation – Hebrews 13:7-8

DECEMBER 28

Meditation and the mind

*... I meditate on all your works and
consider what your hands have done.*
Psalm 143:5

*O*ver the years I have found through talking to
Christians – especially the well educated – that
they fear bringing their minds under the authority
of Christ is a denial of their rationality. But submitting to Christ's revelation does not mean we
have to stop thinking; it means we think more
effectively. If we do not seek to know more of the
mind of Christ through prayer and biblical
meditation then how can we claim to be Christ's
disciples? *Every* Christian is expected to be a pupil
in the school of Jesus Christ. If we reject this idea
then surely our commitment to him must be in
doubt.

For reading & meditation – Psalm 143:1-12

DECEMBER 29

A humble mind

*Your attitude should be the
same as that of Christ Jesus.*
Philippians 2:5

*W*hat is humility? How can it be defined? The dictionary defines it as "meekness" or "the quality of having or showing a low estimate of one's importance". What surprises many is that humility, generally speaking, is looked down upon by the people of the world. Biblical humility is the attitude of mind that regards the interests of others as more important than one's own. This attitude is missing from much of today's thinking. Believe me, Christianity that does not begin with humility – doesn't begin.

For reading & meditation – Philippians 2:1-11

DECEMBER 30

Outside the camp!

*We have an altar from which those who minister
at the tabernacle have no right to eat.*
Hebrews 13:10

"*L*et us, then, go to him outside the camp," the
writer tells the Hebrew Christians, "bearing the
disgrace he bore" (v. 13). There is a shame at the
heart of the gospel and it must be borne. For some
it may mean family disinheritance. Still others find
their path to professional advancement blocked because of their association with Christ. What do
we do when we find ourselves in this position?
We simply remind ourselves that this world is not
our home. We are simply passing through. We are
heading for an eternal city – the city of God.

For reading & meditation – Hebrews 13:9-14

DECEMBER 31